Assessing and Teaching Reading Comprehension and Writing K-3

Volume 2

K. Michael Hibbard
Elizabeth A. Wagner

EYE ON EDUCATION
6 DEPOT WAY WEST, SUITE 106
LARCHMONT, NY 10538
(914) 833–0551
(914) 833–0761 fax
www.eyeoneducation.com

For information about permission to reproduce selections from this book, write: Eye On Education, Permissions Dept., Suite 106, 6 Depot Way West, Larchmont, NY 10538.

Library of Congress Cataloging-in-Publication Data

Hibbard, K. Michael.
 Assessing and teaching reading comprehension and writing, K-3 / K. Michael Hibbard,
  Elizabeth A. Wagner
   p. cm.
  Includes bibliographical references.
  ISBN 1-930556-43-8
   1. Language arts (Early childhood)--Ability testing. 2. Reading comprehension--Ability testing. I. Wagner, Elizabeth A., 1950- II. Title.

 LB1139.5.L35 H54 2003
 372.6049--dc21   2002072150

10 9 8 7 6 5 4 3 2 1

Editorial and production services provided by
Richard H. Adin Freelance Editorial Services
52 Oakwood Blvd., Poughkeepsie, NY 12603-4112
(845-471-3566)

Also Available from EYE ON EDUCATION

**Assessing and Teaching
Reading Comprehension and Pre-Writing K-3, Volume 1**
by K. Michael Hibbard and Elizabeth A. Wagner

**Beyond Stories:
Young Children's Nonfiction Composition**
by Susan Britsch

**Reading, Writing, and Gender:
Instructional Strategies and Classroom Activities
That Work for Girls and Boys**
by Gail Goldberg and Barbara Roswell

**Teaching, Learning and Assessment Together:
The Reflective Classroom**
by Arthur K. Ellis

Technology Tools for Young Learners
by Leni von Blanckensee

**Buddies:
Reading, Writing, and Math Lessons**
by Pia Hansen Powell

**Better Instruction Through Assessment:
What Your Students Are Trying to Tell You**
by Leslie Walker Wilson

Assessment Portfolios for Elementary Students
Milwaukee Public Schools

**Open-Ended Questions in Elementary Mathematics:
Instruction and Assessment**
by Mary Kay Dyer and Christine Moynihan

**A Collection of Performance Tasks and Rubrics
Primary School Mathematics**
by Charlotte Danielson and Pia Hansen

**A Collection of Performance Tasks and Rubrics
Upper Elementary School Mathematics**
by Charlotte Danielson

**Mathematics the Write Way:
Activities for Every Elementary Classroom**
by Marilyn S. Neil

Teacher Retention
What is Your Weakest Link?
by India J. Podsen

Coaching and Mentoring First-Year and Student Teachers
by India J. Podsen and Vicki M. Denmark

Handbook on Teacher Portfolios
for Evaluation and Professional Development
by Pamela D. Tucker, James H. Stronge,
and Christopher R. Gareis

The School Portfolio Toolkit
A Planning, Implementation, and Evaluation Guide
for Continuous School Improvement
by Victoria L. Bernhardt

Data Analysis for Comprehensive Schoolwide Improvement
by Victoria L. Bernhardt

Navigating Comprehensive School Change:
A Guide for the Perplexed
by Thomas G. Chenoweth and Robert B. Everhart

Dealing With Difficult Teachers, 2d ed.
by Todd Whitaker

Motivating and Inspiring Teachers:
The Educational Leader's Guide for Building Staff Morale
by Todd Whitaker, Beth Whitaker, and Dale Lumpa

Teaching Matters
Motivating & Inspiring Yourself
by Todd and Beth Whitaker

Feeling Great! The Educator's Guide for
Eating Better, Exercising Smarter, and Feeling Your Best
by Todd Whitaker& Jason Winkle

What Great Principals Do Differently:
Fifteen Things That Matter Most
by Todd Whitaker

Dealing With Difficult Parents
(And With Parents in Difficult Situations)
by Todd Whitaker and Douglas J. Fiore

Bouncing Back!
How Your School Can Succeed in the Face of Adversity
by Jerry Patterson, Janice Patterson, & Loucrecia Collins

Table of Contents

1

A Roadmap to This Book

Objectives for This Chapter

♦ An overview of this book.
♦ Connections between the Standards for the Assessment of Reading and Writing by the National Council of Teachers of English and the International Reading Association, and the strategies presented in this book.

A Graphic Overview of This Book

Figure 1.1 presents a graphic that highlights the contents of this book. Students use thinking skills and reading comprehension strategies to interact with texts, connect those texts to other texts and to personal experiences. They reveal their comprehension through speaking, drawing, graphic organizers, and writing.

Authentic performance tasks are created to engage students with fiction and nonfiction texts and use thinking skills such as sequencing, listing, describing, categorizing, inferring, predicting, comparing, contrasting, judging and evaluating. The performance tasks ask the students to discuss what they have learned; draw and label pictures; put information into a wide range of graphic organizers; and write sentences, narrative and expository paragraphs, multiparagraph stories, and multiparagraph expository pieces.

The first volume in this two-set series titled, *Assessing and Teaching Reading Comprehension and Pre-Writing, K–3*, provides a good foundation for this second book.

Assessment tools including assessment lists, analytic rubrics, and holistic rubrics are used to assess and evaluate this type of student work.

Figure 1.1 shows that following classroom routines, following directions, working cooperatively with others, and self-assessment create a foundation for the improvement of language arts skills. Self-assessment is an essential part of the strategies presented in this book and is introduced through helping students improve their behavior in the classroom. Self-assessment is a major component of all the performance tasks in this book.

The Topics for Each Chapter

Figure 1.2 presents the topics for each chapter.

Figure 1.1. Revealing Reading Comprehension through Speaking, Drawing, Graphic Organizers and Writing

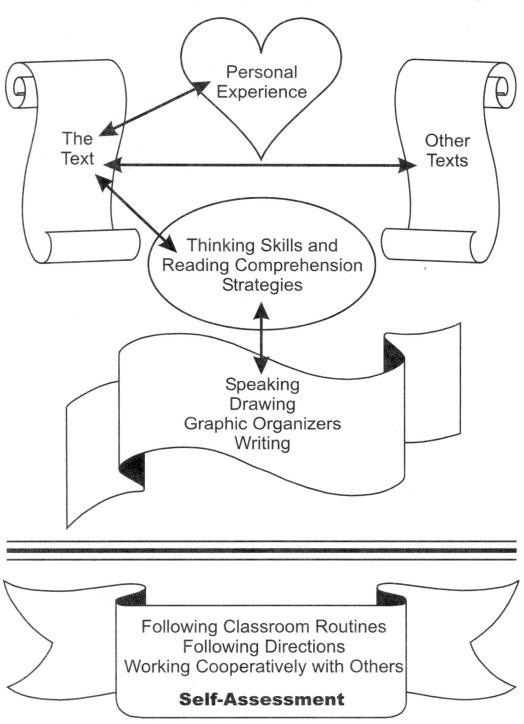

Figure 1.2. Topics for Each Chapter

Chapter Number	Chapter Title	Topics
1	**A Roadmap To This Book**	• An overview of this book. • Connections between the Standards for the Assessment of Reading and Writing by the National Council of Teachers of English and the International Reading Association, and the strategies presented in this book.
2	**Teaching and Assessing Reading Comprehension Through Writing Sentences, Paragraphs, Stories, and Multiparagraph Expository Writing**	• The relationship among thinking-skill verbs, graphic organizers and the writing process. • A framework that defines the traits of writing. • Strategies to create performance tasks that use the writing process to teach and assess reading comprehension. • Strategies to create assessment tools to assess the quality of student's use of writing to show understanding of what was read.
3	**Assessment Tools and Performance Tasks For Writing**	• Graphic organizers for pre-writing • Assessment tools for writing • Performance tasks for leveled books
4	**Teaching and Assessing Reading Comprehension Through Retelling**	• Strategies to generate questions to engage the student in retelling. • Scoring tools for retelling. • Strategies to use the questions and scoring tools for benchmark books.
5	**Connecting Standards and Themes To Performance Tasks**	• Connections among English Language Arts standards, performance tasks, and assessment lists used to teach and assess reading comprehension. • Strategies to use themes and essential questions for literature and disciplines, such as science and social studies, are used to help create performance tasks.

Standards for the Assessment of Reading and Writing

The following pages are a summary of the standards from the book entitled, *Standards for the Assessment of Reading and Writing*, 1994, International Reading Association and the National Council of Teachers of English, ISBN 0-87207-674-1. The description of the connections between the standards, and the materials and strategies presented in this book follow.

Standard 1: The Interests of the Student Are Paramount in Assessment

Summary of Standard 1	Connection between the Standard and the Materials and Strategies of This Book
The purpose of assessment is to improve student performance. The very process of assessing reading comprehension and writing should make the student a better reader and writer. Reading and writing are used to find and communicate information, ideas, and feelings. Assessment should be authentic and focus on how well students use reading and writing to learn and communicate. Finally, because the assessment process includes opportunities for the student to assess and evaluate the quality of their work, the assessment process helps the student become a reflective learner.	The performance tasks presented in this book are authentic opportunities for students to use reading and writing for learning and communication. Each performance task is built around thinking-skill verbs and components of the writing process. The assessment lists are derived from rubrics related to speaking, drawing, using graphic organizers, and writing. The performance tasks are embedded in units of instruction to serve as learning activities and opportunities to assess student performance. Each performance task has an assessment list that is used before, during, and after a task is completed to assess the quality of a student's work.

Standard 2: The Primary Purpose of Assessment Is to Improve Teaching and Learning

Summary of Standard 2	Connection between the Standard and the Materials and Strategies of This Book
The interests of the student are served if teaching and learning improves. This standard emphasizes the importance of reflection by both the student and the teacher. Through self-reflection, the learner identifies strengths and weaknesses and then sets and carries out goals to improve their own performance. Likewise, through self-reflection, the teacher identifies strengths and weaknesses of the materials and strategies of teaching and works to improve both. The assessment process must foster this self-reflection and improvement on the part of both student and teacher.	Self-assessment helps students learn to pay attention and take responsibility for the quality of their work. Analytic and holistic rubrics for drawing, speaking, and using graphic organizers are found in volume one of this two-set series, *Assessing and Teaching Reading Comprehension and Pre-Writing K–3*. Analytic and holistic rubrics for various types of writing are found in this book. These assessment tools provide a source of information for teachers to use to gain information about student performance. Teachers assess the students' work and the quality of their self-assessment through the use of assessment lists and rubrics. The information from using assessment lists and rubrics becomes the basis for plans to improve instruction.

Standard 3: Assessment Must Reflect and Enable Critical Inquiry into Curriculum and Instruction

Summary of Standard 3	Connection between the Standard and the Materials and Strategies of This Book
Because reading and writing are complex acts used in very flexible ways, curriculum should plan for the use of reading and writing for these authentic purposes. The curriculum must also include assessments that are well-suited to authentic purposes of reading and writing. Analysis and reflection on the data from assessments helps the teacher decide if the curriculum and assessments are encouraging the use of reading and writing as authentic tools for learning.	Each performance task is an authentic use of reading and writing for the purposes of learning and communicating. Each performance task asks the student to produce a product for a specific audience. Students are learning that reading and writing serves to answer their own questions and also to teach, inform, or entertain an audience. Teachers evaluate the success of performance tasks as authentic opportunities to use reading and writing.

Standard 4: Assessment Must Recognize and Reflect the Intellectually And Socially Complex Nature of Reading and Writing and the Important Roles of School, Home, and Society in Literacy Development

Summary of Standard 4	Connection between the Standard and the Materials and Strategies of This Book
Reading and writing are such complex acts that no one type of assessment is sufficient. Therefore, a set of carefully chosen assessments should be used. These assessments must include opportunities for students to show how well they can use reading and writing for authentic learning and communication. In addition, data from these assessments should not be reduced to a single rating or score.	Performance tasks should be one component in a balanced literacy assessment plan. Teachers and administrators should work together to use a set of assessments that helps the classroom teacher make decisions to improve instruction. The assessment lists and analytic rubrics used in this book provide information about the specific strengths and weaknesses of each student.

Standard 5: Assessment Must Be Fair and Equitable

Summary of Standard 5	Connection between the Standard and the Materials and Strategies of This Book
Assessments must be free of cultural bias and students must have a reasonable opportunity to learn what is to be assessed.	Performance tasks and assessment tools are created and modified by teachers to be fair and equitable to students. Teachers select a performance task to use and then plan instruction to help students learn what the performance task will ask them to do. Therefore the students will have many opportunities to learn the content of what will be assessed.

Standard 6: The Consequences of an Assessment Procedure Are the First, and the Most Important, Consideration in Establishing the Validity of the Assessment

Summary of Standard 6	Connection between the Standard and the Materials and Strategies of This Book
Assessment must help to improve student performance in the authentic use of reading and writing for learning and communication. A set of assessments would include both tests for specific skills and assessments of how well students read and write to learn and communicate. Including performance assessments in the assessment plan will encourage teachers to use reading and writing in the classroom for authentic purposes. Assessments should help classroom teachers make day-to-day decisions that help adjust and differentiate their materials and strategies to improve the performance of all students. The amount of time spent in assessment must be balanced with the time spent using data from assessment to teach and learn.	Performance tasks and assessment tools are one component of instruction in balance with other classroom activities. The assessment lists provide an efficient way for the teacher to communicate expectations to students and to assess their performance. The performance tasks are worth the time they take. Performance tasks ask students to use knowledge and language arts skills in the context of constructing thoughts and communicating them to others. Classroom instruction that precedes the performance tasks focus both on specific skills and how to use them to solve real learning and communications problems.

Standard 7: The Teacher Is the Most Important Agent of Assessment

Summary of Standard 7	Connection between the Standard and the Materials and Strategies of This Book
First and foremost, teachers should be readers and writers. They should continuously improve their knowledge of the research and best practices of reading and writing. Some of the best professional development occurs when teachers discuss and share judgments about student work and plan materials and strategies to improve student performance.	Conversations about student work, as discussed through the lens of assessment lists and rubrics is excellent professional development. Based on what they learn, teachers plan improvements in performance tasks and their supporting materials. Learning to modify existing performance tasks and assessment lists, and to collaborate in designing new tasks, help teachers learn more about the content and process skills in their disciplines.

Standard 8: The Assessment Process Should Involve Multiple Perspectives and Sources of Data.

Summary of Standard 5	Connection between the Standard and the Materials and Strategies of This Book
A variety of assessments must be used to take a comprehensive look at student performance. Anecdotal Records, Running Records with Retelling, High Frequency Words, Letter Name Inventory, Letter Sound Inventory, Developmental Spelling, Dictation, the Gates MacGinitie Reading Test, and Performance Tasks as presented in this book are examples of assessment to consider. There should be a balance between assessment of skill and assessments of authentic use of reading and writing for learning and communication.	Performance tasks are only one component of a balanced assessment plan that includes other tests, such as running records, retelling, and teacher observations.

Standard 9: Assessment Must Be Based in the School Community

Summary of Standard 9	Connection between the Standard and the Materials and Strategies of This Book
It is important for educators, parents, and other members of the community to talk with one another to understand and communicate how reading and writing are rich, complex, flexible tools people use to learn and communicate. The school's curriculum, instructional practices, and assessments all work together to reflect an understanding of reading and writing. This common understanding will help a partnership flourish among educators, parents, and other community members.	Performance tasks and assessment lists are excellent ways to show parents how reading and writing are tools for learning. Student work accompanied by an assessment list that has been used by the student, and by the teacher to assess the quality of the self-assessment and the student work is valued by parents. Performance tasks, assessment lists, and student work are excellent materials for parent conferences.

Standard 10: All Members of the Educational Community—Students, Parents, Teachers, Administrators, Policy Makers, and the Public—Must Have a Voice in the Development, Interpretation, and Reporting of Assessment

Summary of Standard 10	Connection between the Standard and the Materials and Strategies of This Book
Educators, parents, and other members of the educational community engage in a dialogue that reflects and defines the understanding of how the data will be communicated to the public. The outcome of this process is that parents are well-informed about their children's performance in reading and writing and are happy with the work that teachers are doing to improve performance.	The use of performance tasks and assessment lists as one component of teaching and assessment must be explained to the Board of Education, parents, and others. The authentic nature of performance tasks makes them very appealing to all concerned audiences. It is important to show how data on student performance is generated from performance tasks and how it is used to drive instruction. Finally, it is important to show improvements in student performance over time.

Standard 11: Parents Must Be Involved As Active, Essential Participants in the Assessment Process.

Summary of Standard 11	Connection between the Standard and the Materials and Strategies of This Book
Schools need to reach out to parents in a wide variety of ways that respond to the diverse needs and life commitments of the families. Reporting procedures such as report cards, parent conferences, portfolios, and letters from the school accompanying state test data reports should be planned in collaboration with parents. Parents should also be encouraged to participate in professional development offerings.	Performance tasks and student work can become a central part of parent conferences, portfolio exhibitions, and other parent meetings. Performance tasks and assessment lists are easy ways to teach parents about what is important in teaching and learning.

2

Teaching and Assessing Reading Comprehension through Writing Sentences, Paragraphs, Stories, and Multiparagraph Expository Writing

Topics in This Chapter

- The relationship among thinking-skill verbs, graphic organizers and the writing process.
- A framework that defines the traits of writing.
- Strategies to create performance tasks that use the writing process to teach and assess reading comprehension.
- Strategies to create assessment tools to assess the quality of student's use of writing to show understanding of what was read.

Reading Is a Developmental Process

Books that are at the appropriate level of difficulty for each student are an essential element of an early literacy program. Because there is a range of reading comprehension levels among the students in a class, there needs to be a range of books for them to use during instruction and also for independent reading. Sets of leveled books are now common in elementary schools.

Leveled Books

The system of leveling books used in this chapter was developed by Irene C. Fountas and Gay Su Pinnell in their book *Guided Reading Good First Teaching for All Children*, 1996, Portsmouth, NH, Heinemann.

According to Fountas and Pinnell, "Leveled books are books put into a continuum based on the combination of variables that support and confirm readers' strategic actions and offer the problem-solving opportunities that build the reading process. These variables include length, size and layout of the format, vocabulary and concepts, language structure, text structure and genre, predictability and pattern of language, and illustration support."

Leveled Books and Grade Level

Reading is a highly developmental process, and students in any one primary classroom vary greatly on the continuum of becoming readers. The teacher selects an appropriately leveled book for each student. Students working at the same level may be grouped together temporarily.

Because there is a continuum of reading ability in a classroom, a continuum of leveled books is used. Generally, levels A through C support the development of readers in kindergarten. Levels A through I support the development of readers in grade one. Levels B through P support the development of readers in grade two, and levels I through P support the development of readers in grade three. In some cases, students as young as first graders may be advanced readers capable of reading level P with good comprehension.

Books Used with This Chapter

Leveled books are becoming a common component of an early balanced literacy program, and this chapter shows how to use leveled books as the basis for creating performance tasks to teach and assess reading comprehension. Figure 2.1 correlates a specific level with a book used in this chapter.

Figure 2.1. Leveled Books Used in This Chapter

Level	Book
A	Carle, E. (1987). *Have You Seen My Cat?* New York: Simon & Schuster.
B	Butler, K. T. (2000). *We Are Friends* (M. Grejniec, Illus.). New York: Harcourt.
C	Butler, T. (2000). *Happy Birthday* (P. Paparone, Illus.). New York: Harcourt.
D	Satin Capucilli, A. (1996). *Biscuit* (pictures by P. Schories). New York: HaperCollins.
D-E	Buck, N. (1996). *Sid and Sam* (pictures by G. B. Karas). New York: Harcourt.
E-F	McPhail, D. (2000). *Big Brown Bear.* New York: Harcourt.
G	Simon, N. (1995). *Fire Fighters* (P. Paparone, Illus.). New York: Simon & Schuster.
H	Branley, F. M. (1962). *The Big Dipper* (M. Coxe, Illus.). New York: HarperCollins.
I	Manushkin, F. (1994). *Peeping and Sleeping* (J. Plecas, Illus.). New York: Houghton Mifflin.
J-K	Rylant, C. (1990). *Henry and Mudge and the Happy Cat* (pictures by S. Stevenson). New York: Simon & Schuster.
J-K	Suen, A. (1997). *Man on the Moon* (B. Huang, Illus.). New York: Viking Children's Books.
K	Hoban, R. (1970). *A Bargain for Frances* (pictures by L. Hoban). New York: Harper Row.
L	Van Leeuwen, J. (1994). *Amanda Pig and Her Big Brother Oliver* (pictures by A. Schweninger). New York: Puffin Books.
L	Milton, J. (1999). *Dinosaur Days* (R. Roe, Illus.). New York: Random House.
L	Marshall, J.(1985) *Miss Nelson Has a Field Day.* New York: Scholastic.
M	Williams, V. B. (1982). *A Chair For My Mother.* New York: William Morrow.

M	Williams, V. B. (1991) *Cherries and Cherry Pits.* New York: William Morrow.
M	Pope Osborne, M. (1996). *Midnight on the Moon.* New York: Scholastic.
M	Aardema, V. (1975). *Why Mosquitoes Buzz in People's Ears* (pictures by L. Dillon & D. Dillon). New York: Dial Books for Young Readers.
N	O'Connor, J. (1998). *Jackie Robinson.* New York: Random House.
O	Yolen, J. (1987). *Owl Moon* (J. Schoenherr, Illus.). New York: Scholastic.
P	Ballard, R. D. (1993). *Finding the Titanic.* Toronto, Canada: Madison Press.
P	Cole, J. (1999). *The Search For The Missing Bones* (B. Degen, Illus.). New York: Scholastic.

A Student's Work Reveals His or Her Level of Reading Comprehension

The nature and degree of a student's reading comprehension can be revealed by observing a student's drawing, speaking, use of information graphic organizers, and writing. The first book in this two-set series, *Assessing and Teaching Reading Comprehension and Pre-Writing, K–3*, focuses on drawing, speaking, and graphic organizers. This book focuses on writing.

Writing Process

Beginning in the primary grades, writing becomes one of the most important ways that reading comprehension is taught and assessed. The process of thinking about what was read is translated into the process of writing.

Writing is a process of learning through constructing complete thoughts on paper. Thinking becomes explicit when it is transformed into complete sentences. In thinking-skill tasks that ask for Initial Understanding, the student works at explicitly putting information from the text into written language. Here, the student might be asked to list events in the order in which they occur, state the setting for the story, and name the characters. In thinking-skill tasks that ask for higher-order thinking, such as Developing an Interpretation, Making Connections, and Critical Stance, the student works even harder to make inferences, predictions, comparisons, and judgments. Then, the student works to select, organize and put information into a logical order in a sentence, paragraph, or multiparagraph piece.

When students use a systematic process when they write, they are more likely to think and write clearly. Figure 2.2 presents a graphic for the process of writing and each of the five steps are described here.

1. **Pre-Writing**: The student writer is thinking about what he or she already knows about the topic and may draw or write it down in a graphic organizer.

The student may also do research that includes rereading a story, looking at pictures, and reading nonfiction material. The student may also get information by talking to other students and the teacher. This new information may be added to the graphic organizer.

The first book in this two-set series, *Assessing and Teaching Reading Comprehension and Pre-Writing, K–3*, focuses on oral descriptions, drawing, and the use of graphic organizers, which includes words and phrases. This book shows the progression that enables the student to successfully write sentences, paragraphs, and multiparagraphs. The drawings and graphic organizers that are the focus of the first book become pre-writing activities that help the students organize their thoughts to achieve more complex writing.

2. **Drafting**: In this step the student writes a first draft of the sentence, paragraph, or longer piece. Simple tasks for beginning writers ask for a sentence. As students become more capable writers, longer passages are required. Performance tasks in this chapter will include those asking for a sentence and those asking for a paragraph. Multiparagraph writing will be a focus in later grades. Most writing in the early grades is first-draft writing.

3. **Revising**: Occasionally, the teacher may ask the student to continue working on a sentence or a paragraph. Revision is more common starting in second grade.

After the first draft is completed, the student uses the assessment list to assess his or her own work. The teacher uses the assessment list to give the student feedback both on the quality of the writing and the accuracy of the self-assessment. If the teacher has decided that the writing will go through one or more revision cycles, the student uses the feedback from the self-assessment and teacher assessment to improve the writing.

4. **Editing**: Occasionally, the teacher may ask the student to check the spelling of a word. The student dictionary, the word wall, and the word web are tools for the student. Other editing can include checking the use of capitalization and ending punctuation. Care must be taken not to overdo editing in the early years of writing.

5. **Publishing**: When the writing is complete, it is sent to its intended audience such as the Principal, a person at their home, another student in the school, a pen pal, or a visitor to the student's school or classroom. If there is no specific audience, the work may be published in the room or on one of the school's bulletin boards. In some schools, grade levels or the whole school meet regularly to share the writing of students at various grade levels. The writing can be accompanied by drawings and/or graphic organizers.

Figure 2.2. Five Steps in the Process of Writing

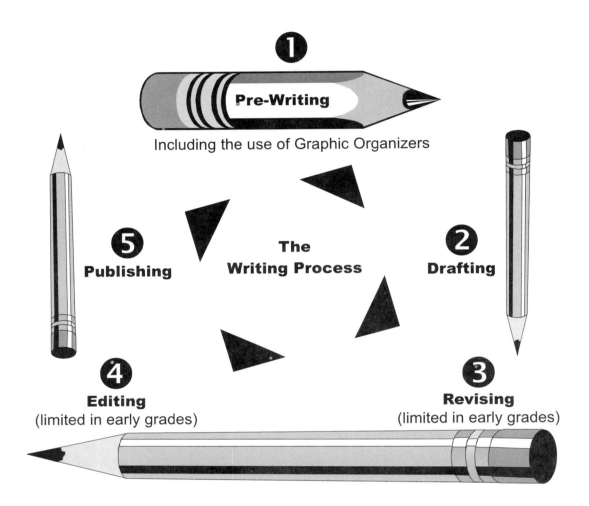

Thinking-Skill Verbs and Reading Comprehension

The National Assessment of Education Progress (NEAP) developed a framework that describes four tpes of reading comprehension, as shown in Figure 2.3.

Figure 2.3. Four Levels of Reading Comprehension

Level of Reading Comprehension	Description of the Level	Verbs Used with the Level, Including
Initial Understanding (IU)	The student is asked to retell factual information from the fiction or nonfiction text.	List, Describe, Sequence, Name
Developing an Interpretation (DI)	The student is asked to show higher-level thinking in processing information from one story or part of a nonfiction text. The differences between DI and MC is that in DI, the student is focusing on one information source, whereas in MC, the student is focusing on two or more information sources.	Infer, Predict, Generalize, Analyze, Explain
Making Connections (MC)	The student is asked to show higher-level thinking in processing information from the text and to connect that information to his own experience (text to self), the everyday world (text to world) and/or information from other texts (text to text.)	Compare, Contrast, Infer, Predict, Generalize, Analyze, Explain
Critical Stance (CS)	For fiction, the student is asked to critique the work of the author and/or illustrator regarding how well they did their work to create an effective story. For example, the student might be asked to evaluate how well the author used descriptive language to tell the story and to support his opinion with examples from the text. For nonfiction, the student is asked to judge the quality of an information source. Here the student might be asked to determine if the information in the book is on the desired topic, is accurate, is written by a qualified author, and unbiased.	Evaluate, Judge, Rate

The first volume of this two-set series, *Assessing and Teaching Reading Comprehension and Pre-Writing Activities, K–3*, provides an extensive discussion of these four levels of reading comprehension.

Thinking-Skill Verbs and Pre-Writing

Each verb in the reading comprehension framework calls for a certain type of information processing. Sequencing, listing, inferring, predicting, comparing, contrasting, evaluating, and rating each require different ways to organize information. Graphic organizers help students organize and structure their thinking. The first volume of this two-set series provides an extensive discussion of how to use graphic organizers. A collection of graphic organizers and performance tasks that use them are also presented in volume one.

The completed graphic organizers then help prepare them for more complex writing.

Behaviors That Support Writing

Figures 2.4 and 2.5 shows the use of a "T" chart to identify the behaviors that writers use and the ways that writing is supported in the classroom. Elements from these "T" charts can be the basis of class discussions and interactive writing activities, mini-lessons with individuals or small groups, or incorporated into assessment lists for performance tasks that ask for writing.

The first volume in this two-set series, *Assessing and Teaching Reading Comprehension and Pre-Writing Activities, K–3*, devotes a chapter to the use of "T" charts to create assessment lists to teach and assess classroom routines, following directions, and encouraging a friend to participate.

Figure 2.4. "T" Chart for A Good Writing Job

When I do a good job of writing

it looks like:	*it sounds like:*
The book is on my desk.	Using my whisper voice to sound out a word.
Looking at the cover and pictures in the book.	Using my whisper voice to read and reread a sentence.
Moving from page to page in the book.	Reading to a buddy.
Sometimes I am thinking quietly.	Talking with a buddy about ideas.
Looking at the word wall.	Using my large group-sharing voice to read my writing.
Doing a word search in the book.	
My mouth is moving when I sound out words.	
Using my personal dictionary.	
Looking at the assessment list.	
Drawing pictures.	
Writing labels on the picture.	
Putting words in graphic organizers.	
Writing.	
Using a word spacer to keep spaces between my words.	
Making changes in my writing.	
Looking at the assessment list and checking my work.	
I am working on my portfolio.	

Figure 2.5. "T" Chart for Encouragement from Classroom

When our classroom encourages us all to be writers,

it looks like:	*it sounds like:*
Student writing displayed on the wall.	We say encouraging things to each other during interactive writing.
Student work on the school bulletin boards.	We are quiet when someone else is reading what they write.
All students have their work displayed.	We read what we write to a buddy.
Displays changed often.	We read what we write to our group or to the whole class.
Drawings and graphic organizers displayed along with the writing.	Our teacher says encouraging things to us.
Assessment lists that show self-assessment displayed with the writing.	Our teacher talks with us about items on our assessment lists.
All kinds of writing displayed.	Our teacher reads his or her writing to us.
Words on the word wall.	We read our writing to the principal and other adults in the school.
Words on the word webs in the centers.	The principal comes into our room and talks to us about our writing.
Personal dictionary is used.	Other adults in the school come into our room and talk with us about our writing.
Watching the teacher model how to plan writing.	We go to other classrooms to read our writing to other students.
Looking at the benchmarks.	We go to the principal's office to read our writing.
Taking turns during interactive writing.	We read our writing to students during the school's Town Meeting.
Students talking with other students about their writing.	We read our writing to our parents.
Students talking with teachers about their writing and the assessment list.	
Students reading their writing to their buddies and to students in groups.	
Going into other classrooms to read our writing.	
We are working in our portfolio.	

Traits of Writing

There are many traits of writing to look at regarding the quality of student writing. These traits of writing will become the basis for the creation of analytic rubrics, holistic rubrics, and assessment lists to examine the strengths and weaknesses of student writing and to plan subsequent instruction to focus teaching and improve student performance.

- **Main Idea**: The main idea is the central point of the writing. When the writing is only one sentence, that sentence is the main idea. When the writing is several sentences, one should be a statement of what the paragraph is about. Main idea sentences usually come at the beginning of the paragraph in the early grades.

  The main idea of the writing should be clear and accurate according to the writing task. Main ideas that are clear but off-topic are, of course, not terrific work.

  A main idea is relevant to expository writing. The equivalent to the main idea in narrative writing is "theme."

- **Problem–Solution**: This trait for narrative writing concerns the development of a problem in the first part of the story and a solution or resolution to that problem in the end. Actions including complications occur between the presentation of the problem and its resolution. Sometimes, the Problem–Solution is called the "Conflict and Resolution." Problems and their Solutions can be used in both fiction and nonfiction writing.

- **Character**: Narrative writing includes a character, which could be the student. An animal can be a character in a story. More than one character can be developed. Nonfiction writing can include real people, animals, and other things.

- **Setting**: Narrative writing also includes a place or location in which the character(s) take(s) action. Settings are important to some kinds of nonfiction writing, such as news reporting and journals of real experiences and events.

- **Dialogue**: Dialogue is verbal interaction between characters and is used to develop the characters and/or the theme or plot of the story. Advancing writers at this grade level attempt dialogue. Dialogue is a literary device often used in fiction and it can also be used in nonfiction such as news reporting. Dialogue in the form of quotes is often used in persuasive writing.

- **Supporting Details**: When the writing is only one sentence, the details are the "describing words," i.e., adjectives, used in that sentence. When the writing is a paragraph, the details are both the describing words in the main idea sentence and in the sentences that follow. Supporting details must be appropriate to the main idea they are elaborating. Some teachers ask students to include three supporting details for a main idea.

A web graphic organizer with a space for the main idea with three radiating lines for supporting details is helpful to students as a reminder to have both a main idea and supporting details.

+ **Organization**: When the writing is only one sentence, organization is not relevant. When the writing is a paragraph, the main idea may come first and then supporting details are presented in some logical order. If the paragraph is presenting a sequence, then the supporting details should accurately represent the sequence.

In narrative writing, organization is established through the structure of "beginning, middle, and ending."

In expository writing, the main idea is presented first and then subsequent sentences or paragraphs provide elaboration and support of that main idea.

+ **Transition Words**: Words such as "first, second, third, next, then, last, and, and because" help link ideas and actions so that writing flows smoothly.

+ **Focus**: When the writing is focused, it is on the topic. When a sentence is well-focused it is exactly on the assignment. When a paragraph is well-focused, all of its sentences are on the topic.

+ **Sentence Structure**: One aspect of sentence structure is whether the sentence is complete or only a fragment. Another aspect of sentence structure is whether it is simple, compound, or complex. A variety of correct sentences adds interest to the writing.

+ **Vocabulary**: Vocabulary is word choice. Students should choose words that are vivid, accurate according to the topic of their writing, and interesting to their audience. Vocabulary should be multisensory, e.g., words that appeal to the senses of sight, hearing, smell, touch, and taste.

+ **Mechanics**: Mechanics include spelling, beginning capitalization, and ending punctuation.

+ **Presentability and Neatness**: Students are expected to work on their penmanship and overall appearance of their work.

The Options for Assessment Tools

Assessment tools include analytic and holistic rubrics and assessment lists. Figure 2.6 presents the "Assessment Tool Tree." The traits of writing form the trunk, which provides the common starting point for the development of all assessment tools for writing. The source of the traits of writing are the roots which represent the Curriculum Standards (Language Arts), actual writing done by people in their jobs and everyday lives, and the samples of student work selected to define the goals for performance.

Once the traits of writing have been identified, assessment tools can be created. Analytic rubrics are often developed first, followed by the development of holistic rubrics. These rubrics remain static and constant for several years and are used by teachers at several grade levels. The analytic and holistic rubrics are used in two ways. First, they are used at regular intervals during the year to assess student work. Secondly, they are used to help create assessment lists that are used more frequently.

The description of the highest levels of performance in an analytic rubric provide the ideas for items for assessment lists. Teachers tailor assessment lists to specific books. They also plan the wording and number of items to be appropriate to the experience and needs of their students. Assessment lists are changed as needed. The assessment lists always contain one or two items called, "Sure Things" because those items relate to some aspect of writing that the teacher knows the students do well. The assessment lists also contain a "Challenge" item that is related to some aspect of writing on which the students are not proficient. These assessment lists help the students confirm and practice what they do well, and to pay attention to something about their writing on which they should improve.

The first volume in this two-set series, *Assessing and Teaching Reading Comprehension and Pre-Writing, K–3*, describes how to make assessment lists and use them with students.

Analytic and Holistic Rubrics for Writing Narrative and Expository Paragraphs

(The rubrics described here are found in Chapter 3.)

When students are comfortable writing sentences, performance tasks asking for paragraphs can be used. Figures 3.4 and 3.5 present analytic rubrics for narrative and expository paragraphs. Figures 3.6 and 3.7 present holistic rubrics for assessing these paragraphs.

Figure 2.6. Assessment Tool Tree

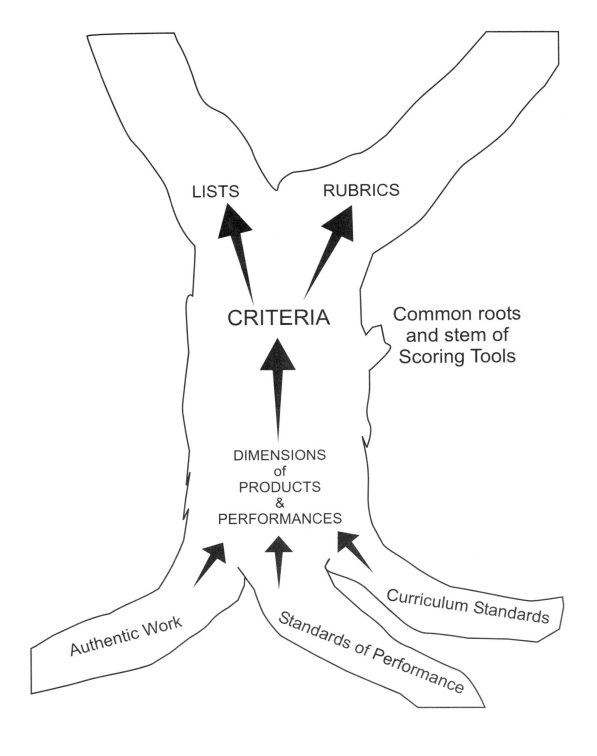

Assessment tools have several uses. First, they provide a "menu" of ideas about writing that can help the teacher create short, focused assessment lists for performance tasks requiring students to write narrative or expository paragraphs. Second, the rubrics can be used to assess the specific strengths and weaknesses of individual students and the whole class. This knowledge can help shape subsequent instruction. Finally, the assessment tools help the teacher communicate with other teachers, the students, and their parents about the strengths and needs of student writers.

Analytic and Holistic Rubrics for Narrative and Expository Multiparagraph Writing

(The rubrics described here are found in Chapter 3.)

Figures 3.8 and 3.9 present analytic rubrics for narrative and expository writing. These analytic rubrics are used to assess the strengths and weaknesses of individuals and the whole group so that instruction can be planned to improve writing. Elements from the analytic rubric can be used to create items for assessment lists.

Figures 3.10 and 3.11 present holistic rubrics for narrative and expository writing. Holistic rubrics are used to assess the "overall" performance of a student and to get an "overall" picture of writing in the classroom.

Again, these analytic and holistic rubrics have three purposes. First, they provide the teacher with a menu of ideas for assessment lists. Second, they help the teacher identify the strengths and weaknesses of individual students, and the overall strengths and weaknesses of the class to improve instruction. And third, they help the teacher communicate with other teachers, administrators, students, and parents.

Using Benchmarks for Student Writing

There are two tools that are needed to define the goals for the quality of student work. The first tool is a scoring tool, such as the analytic rubric. The second tool is actual samples of student work that show what work looks likes at a specific level of quality. Student work at a specific level of quality is called a "benchmark" for that level. Figure 2.7 presents a chart that shows what kinds of student work (drawings, graphic organizers, sentences, narrative paragraphs, expository paragraphs, stories, or multiparagraph expository pieces) is collected and used as benchmarks at each grade level.

In kindergarten, the only benchmarks that are collected are examples of student drawings and graphic organizers. In first grade, drawings, graphic organizers, sentences, and narrative paragraphs are collected. In second grade, drawings, graphic organizers, sentences, narrative paragraphs, and expository paragraphs are collected. Some second-grade students may be ready for multiparagraph stories and expository pieces later during the school. Benchmarks for these written products should be available. In third grade, the focus is on benchmarks for paragraphs and multiparagraph writing.

Benchmarks are needed for whatever type of pre-writing and writing products the students are working on. If a group of second graders is working on drawing, graphic organizers, and sentences, then benchmarks are only needed for those products. If a first grader has developed into an advanced reader and writer, and is ready for a benchmark for a multiparagraph story, then one could be borrowed from the second-grade teacher.

Figure 2.7. Benchmarks for Student Writing

By The End Of Grade	Benchmarks Needed For
K	Drawings
1	Drawings Graphic Organizers Sentences
2	Drawings Graphic Organizers Paragraphs
3	Drawings Graphic Organizers Multi-Paragraph Pieces

Set Targets for Performance without Overwhelming the Students

Notice that Figure 2.8 shows a September through January, and a January through June time frame for each of these four grade levels—kindergarten through grade three. For first grade, only drawings, graphic organizers, and sentences are used as benchmarks during the first half of the school year. Narrative and expository paragraphs are used as benchmarks in winter and spring if the teacher feels that the students are ready to see models of excellence for those more challenging types of writing. The main purpose of using benchmarks is to inspire students to improve their performance, not overwhelm them with seemingly unreachable goals. The introduction of benchmarks for new kinds of student work coincides with their developmental readiness for those new and more challenging types of writing.

The use of specific types of benchmarks in the classroom is coordinated with the use of those products in performance tasks. Performance tasks in grade one during September through January would call for drawings, graphic organizers, and/or sentences as final products. Performance tasks that call for narrative or expository paragraphs would not be used with first graders until the second half of the year. The decision as to when to introduce performance tasks requiring paragraphs is left to the classroom teacher. In March, some first graders may be working on performance tasks that call for narrative paragraphs, whereas other students are working on performance tasks that still only require sentences. By May, most first graders would be working on performance tasks that require paragraphs as their final product. These performance tasks may also call for drawings and/or graphic organizers as a pre-writing first step. In second grade, students continue to use drawings and graphic organizers for pre-writing work, to sharpen their skills in writing paragraphs, and may attempt a few longer pieces. In third grade, work on multiparagraph stories and expository pieces becomes the focus.

Figure 2.8. The Work Students Do Becomes More Challenging Over Time

Time of the Year	Drawings	Graphic Organizers	Sentences	Narrative Paragraphs	Expository Paragraphs	Narrative Stories	Expository Multi-Paragraphs
Jan.–June Grade 3	X	X		X	X	X	X
Sept.–Jan. Grade 3	X	X		X	X	X	X
Jan.–June Grade 2	X	X	X	X	X	X	X
Sept.–Jan. Grade 2	X	X	X	X	X	X	
Jan.–June Grade 1	X	X	X	X	X		
Sept.–Jan. Grade 1	X	X	X				
Jan.–June Kindergarten	X	X					
Sept.–Jan. Kindergarten	X						

Types of Products in Performance Tasks for These Students

Collecting the First Benchmarks to Use

In the beginning, the teacher probably does not have a collection of benchmarks to use. To obtain benchmarks, use performance tasks that call for the type of product for which a benchmark is needed, i.e. a narrative paragraph. With the rubric in hand, look through the student work that results from that task and find two or three pieces that meet the standards to become benchmarks for, in this instance, narrative paragraph. If none of the narrative paragraphs are good enough, provide more instruction and try again. After a few performance tasks, benchmarks can be identified. Teachers working together as a grade level or a pair makes the work of selecting benchmarks more efficient.

Creating Performance Tasks
That Call for Writing

Figure 2.9 presents a plan for using performance tasks that incorporate various types of pre-writing activities and call for different kinds of written final products. In kindergarten, drawings are used as final products of some performance tasks. Some words and phrases may be added to graphic organizers near the end of the year. A few students may begin writing sentences, but they will be the exceptions. Performance tasks calling for sentences usually are not used in the beginning of first grade.

In the beginning of first grade, graphic organizers that ask for a drawing and words are the final products of some performance tasks. When the teacher sees that the students are ready, performance tasks that ask for sentences as final products are introduced. These performance tasks will include drawings and/or graphic organizers as final products. Near the end of first grade, the students may be ready to handle performance tasks that ask for narrative or expository paragraphs of a few sentences each.

Grade two picks up where grade one left off. The student now uses drawings and/or graphic organizers as pre-writing activities for multiparagraph narrative stories or expository writing pieces in the second half of grade two.

In grade three, students continue to use drawings and graphic organizers as pre-writing activities. Some performance tasks will call for paragraphs, but most tasks will ask the student to write multiparagraph stories and expository pieces as the final written products.

This plan could be accelerated or slowed down for individual students or could be based on the readiness of the whole class.

Figure 2.9. Options for the Components of Performance Tasks That Call for a Final Written Product

Pre-Writing Component of Task			Type of Writing as the Final Product		
Reading Ex-perience	*Drawing*	*Graphic Organizer*	*Sentence*	*Paragraph Narrative or Expository Writing*	*Multi-paragraph Story or Expository Writing*
Late Kindergarten	X	X			
Early First Grade	X	X	X		
Later in First Grade	X	X		X	
Early Second Grade	X	X		X	
Later in Second Grade	X	X			X
Early Third Grade	X	X			X
Later in Third Grade	X	X			X

Embedding the Writing Process in the Performance Task

All performance tasks that call for written final products in the early grades will also ask for pre-writing components. When a task calls for a drawing or graphic organizer before a written product, the task will be completed in two steps. First, the students will create and assess the pre-writing work, i.e., the drawing or graphic organizer. Second, the students will write and assess the final product. If both drawing and a graphic organizer are used as pre-writing activities, then the task becomes a three-step task with assessment after each step.

Care must be taken not to make performance tasks too long. The most common problem with performance tasks is that they take too much classroom time. Remember that the performance task is not a "unit of instruction," but only one component of it. Some of the pre-writing activities could be done "before" the performance task is introduced so that the performance task itself requires only one or two periods. When the students are experienced with performance tasks and doing a good job with the shorter ones, longer performance tasks that involve a little research may be introduced.

Specialized Graphic Organizers to Support Multiparagraph Writing

Graphic organizers help students organize information to support their thinking. The first volume of this two-set series, *Assessing and Teaching Reading Comprehension and Pre-Writing, K–3*, presented twenty-nine graphic organizers (GO1 through GO29) used for the thinking-skill verbs "describe, list, sequence, categorize, infer, predict, compare, contrast, evaluate, and rate." These graphic organizers can be the final products of performance tasks or they can be pre-writing activities that prepare students for writing sentences, paragraphs, or multiparagraph stories or expository pieces.

When students are ready to write more complex stories or multiparagraph expository pieces, they may need an additional type of graphic organizer to help them organize and structure their information.

The following fourteen graphic organizers (GO30 through GO43) are useful when preparing students to write stories or multiparagraph expository pieces intended to teach and inform an audience. These graphic organizers are in Chapter 3 of this book.

- ◆ **Story Outline** graphic organizers GO30 through GO37 present structures for getting information ready to write a story.

- ◆ **A Graphic Organizer for Evaluating Nonfiction Texts GO29** is used by students to evaluate the quality of nonfiction books and other resources regarding their usefulness to their research project. This type of evaluation is a very important type of Critical Stance.

- ◆ **Graphic Organizers for Multiparagraph Expository Writing** GO38 through GO43 present structures that help students organize information in preparation for writing multiparagraph expository pieces that are intended to teach and inform the audience.

- ◆ **QKWL Chart** GO38 presents a form students use to begin a research project. The research Question is written in the top box then the student lists what he or she already Knows in the "K" area, lists what he or she Wants to find out in the "W" area, and after the research is completed, summarizes what has been Learned in the "L" area.

Ideas for Performance Tasks That Ask for Writing

Figure 2.10 presents ideas for performance tasks relevant to the leveled books listed at the beginning of this chapter. Leveled books A, B, and C have performance tasks that ask only for drawings. Level D books have a task asking for a graphic organizer. Leveled books E and F have performance tasks that ask for a sentence as a final product. Leveled books G through J have performance tasks that ask for paragraphs and leveled books K through P have performance tasks that ask for multiparagraph writing.

Although there are four tasks for each leveled book, the teacher may not decide to use all four tasks. The teacher decides which tasks and how many tasks to use, based on the time available and the needs of the students. Over the course of several books, the teacher assures that students get a balance of tasks at the Initial Understanding, Developing an Interpretation, Making Connections, and Critical Stance levels of thinking.

The steps to create these ideas include:

- ◆ Select a book at the desired level.

- ◆ Plan for four tasks to cover the four thinking-skill levels Initial Understanding, Developing an Interpretation, Making Connections, and Critical Stance.

- ◆ Select a verb for each task.

- ◆ Create the idea for the task that works with the verb selected.

- ◆ Plan the use of drawing and/or a graphic organizer. If a graphic organizer is to be used, select the specific graphic organizer.

- ◆ For levels F and beyond, select the type of writing to include sentences, paragraph, or multiparagraph pieces.

- ◆ Balance narrative and expository writing.

- ◆ Short performance tasks will only ask for one product, such as a drawing, graphic organizer, or sentence.

- ◆ Longer performance tasks are organized into a series of steps, such as completion of a graphic organizer, the use of an assessment list for the graphic organizer, work on an expository paragraph, and, finally, the use of an assessment list for the written product.

- ◆ Still longer performance tasks will include more steps, each with its own assessment list. These longer tasks will be used occasionally by the most experienced and developmentally ready classes.

- ◆ Generally, even for the older students, most performance tasks should be the short or medium-length versions.

Figure 2.10. Ideas For Performance Tasks For A Continuum Of Leveled Books

IU = Initial Understanding
N = Narrative Writing

DU = Developing an Interpretation
E = Expository Writing

MC = Making Connections
CS = Critical Stance

Level	Book Title	Thinking Skill Verb	Pre-Writing Product		Type of Writing					Idea for Performance Task
			Drawing	Graphic Organizer	Sentence	Paragraph N	Paragraph E	Multi-Paragraph N	Multi-Paragraph E	
A	*Have you seen my cat?*	IU Describe	X							What is this book about?
		DI Infer	X							What did the boy loose?
		MC Compare	X							What does a cat you know look like?
		CS Rate	X							What picture of a cat is the best? Why?
B	*We Are Friends*	IU List	X							What are two things the friends do for fun in this story?
		IU Predict	X							What will the friends do next?
		MC Compare	X							What did the friends do for fun that you like to do for fun?
		CS Evaluate	X							Do you think that the author showed things that kids really like to do? What are those things?

Level	Book Title	Thinking Skill Verb	Pre-Writing Product		Type of Writing						Idea for Performance Task
			Drawing	Graphic Organizer	Sentence	Paragraph		Multi-Paragraph			
						N	E	N	E		
C	Happy Birthday	IU List	X								Who had a birthday?
		DI Infer	X								Did the duck and pig like each other?
		MC Evaluate	X								What is a fun thing you did at your last birthday party?
		CS Evaluate	X								Did the author do a good job of showing activities for birthday parties that are fun? How?
D	Biscuit	IU Describe	X								Who is Biscuit?
		DI Predict	X								What will the little girl and Biscuit do in the morning after they wake up?
		MC Contrast	X								Biscuit did not get into trouble. What would a pet do to get into trouble?
		CS Rate	X								Did the author do a good job of showing how a child and pet can play? How?
E	Sid and Sam	IU Sequence		GO7							How did the story begin? What happened in the middle? How did the story end?
		DI Infer		GO11							What makes Sid and Sam happy?
		MC Contrast		GO22							What do you and your friend do for fun that is different than what Sid and Sam do for fun?
		CS Evaluate		GO26							Was this an interesting story to you? Why?

Level	Book Title	Thinking Skill Verb	Pre-Writing Product: Drawing	Graphic Organizer	Sentence	Paragraph N	Paragraph E	Multi-Paragraph N	Multi-Paragraph E	Idea for Performance Task
F	Big Brown Bear	IU Describe		GO10						What did Big Bear look like?
		DI Predict		GO13	X					Based on the last page of the story, what will happen next?
		MC Compare		GO15	X					What have you done by accident?
		CS Rate		GO24	X					What rating would you give the illustrations in this story? Why?
G	Firefighters	IU Describe		GO14						What do you see, hear, smell, and feel when firemen fight a fire?
		DI Categorize		GO12						What do firemen wear and what tools do they use to fight a fire?
		MC Explain	X		X					What do firemen do that is important to us?
		CS Evaluate		GO27	X					How good a job did the author do of showing that firemen do important jobs?
H	The Big Dipper	DI Describe	X		X					What does the Big Dipper look like?
		DI Infer	X		X					Why is the Big Dipper important?
		MC Compare		GO19	X					How is our sun the same as and different from a star in the Big Dipper?
		CS Rate		GO29	X					Was this a good book for your research on stars? Why?

Level	Book Title	Thinking Skill Verb	Pre-Writing Product: Drawing	Graphic Organizer	Sentence	Paragraph N	Paragraph E	Multi-Paragraph N	Multi-Paragraph E	Idea for Performance Task
I	Peeping and Sleeping	IU Describe		GO16						Who is the story about, when does the story take place, and where does the story take place?
		DI Infer		GO9	X					Why was Barry a little scared?
		MC	X		X					Have you ever used your flashlight to find something outside in the dark?
		CS Evaluate		GO25	X					Is this a good title? Why?
J	Henry And Mudge And The Happy Cat	IU Sequence		GO7	X					What happened in the story?
		DI Predict			X					After Henry put the posters up what will happen next?
		MC Compare		GO21	X					Did you ever feel bad about losing a pet?
		CS Rate		GO23	X					What was the most interesting part of this story? Why?
K	A Bargain For Frances	IU Sequence		GO7						What is the beginning, middle, and ending of this story?
		DI Predict		GO13			X			(Based on the page 38 of Thelma in the candy store) What will happen next?
		MC Compare		GO7		X				Write a story about one friend playing a trick on another friend. This could be a story about you.
		CS Evaluate		GO25	X					Is this a good title for this story? Why?

Level	Book Title	Thinking Skill Verb	Pre-Writing Product		Type of Writing					Idea for Performance Task
			Drawing	Graphic Organizer	Sentence	Paragraph N	Paragraph E	Multi-Paragraph N	Multi-Paragraph E	
K	Man On The Moon	IU Sequence		GO6						What is the sequence of events from lift off to landing on the moon?
		DI Infer		GO10						What are some words that would describe the feeling that Neil Armstrong had when he stepped on the moon?
		MC Compare		GO7		X				Write a story and pretend that you were the first child to step on the moon.
		CS Rate		GO29			X			Was this a good book for your research on astronauts? Why?
L	Amanda Pig and Her Big Brother Oliver	DI List		GO9	X					What are four things that Oliver did that Amanda did also?
		DI Explain					X			Why was Amanda always copying what Oliver did?
		MC Compare	X			X				What would you do if you were Mighty Pig?
		CS Evaluate		GO27			X			Did the author do a good job of showing how children in a family play with each other.
L	Dinosaur Days	IU Describe		GO10						What words best describe the dinosaurs?
		DI Categorize & Explain		GO12			X			If you had to put dinosaurs into two categories what would those two categories be? Explain.
		MC Compare		GO7		X				Tell a story about you visiting the time of the dinosaurs.
		CS Evaluate		GO27			X			The author used a picture of a chicken on page 16 and a house on pages 18 and 19. Did the use of the chicken and house help the author explain dinosaurs to you?

Level	Book Title	Thinking Skill Verb	Pre-Writing Product: Drawing	Pre-Writing Product: Graphic Organizer	Type of Writing: Sentence	Paragraph N	Paragraph E	Multi-Paragraph N	Multi-Paragraph E	Idea for Performance Task
L	Miss Nelson Has A Field Day	UI Summarize		GO16			X			Who is the story about, where did it take place, and when did it take place?
		DI Explain		GO15			X			Why did "The Swamp" get such good results?
		MC Predict		GO34		X				Tell a story about how "The Swamp" could get something to work better at your school.
		CS Evaluate		GO27			X			Did the author do a good job of having a surprise ending? How?
M	A Chair For My Mother	IU List	X	GO9						How did the family get money to put into the jar?
		DI Predict		GO34				X		Tell a story about the next thing that the mother saves money to buy.
		MC Compare		GO14 GO34				X		Now that the mother has a chair, tell a story about what you saved money to buy.
		CS Evaluate		GO28					X	Did the author do a good job writing a story that was interesting to you? How?
M	Cherries And Cherry Pits	IU Sequence		GO8					X	Explain the cycle of growing cherries.
		DI Infer		GO15				X		Explain how you know that Bidemmi is creative.
		MC Generalize		GO12				X		What fruit do you love to eat? Tell a story that shows how you would be like Bidemmi.
		CS Rating		GO19			X			How good were the illustrations in helping to tell this story?

Level	Book Title	Thinking Skill Verb	Pre-Writing Product		Type of Writing						Idea for Performance Task
			Drawing	Graphic Organizer	Sentence	Paragraph		Multi-Paragraph			
						N	E	N	E		
M	Midnight On The Moon	IU Describe		GO10							What words describe what it would be like to be on the moon?
		DI Explain		GO36				X			Jack and Annie found out that there was a fifth thing that they had to find to free Morgan le Fay. What was it and how did they get it?
		MC Compare		GO31 GO36				X			Think of a character from another story that could use a magic tree house to solve a problem. Tell a story about how that character would use the magic tree house.
		CS Judge		GO27							Would you want to read other books written by Mary Pope Osborne? Why or Why not?
M	Why Mosquitos Buzz in People's Ears	IU List	X			X					List the animals in this story.
		DI Predict	X	GO6							Add one more animal to the chain of events in this story.
		MC Compare		GO19			X				This story is a fable. What other fables have you read that you liked? How are they the same and different?
		CS Rate		GO24			X				Did the illustrators do a good job of creating pictures that helped tell the story in an interesting way? How?

Level	Book Title	Thinking Skill Verb	Pre-Writing Product		Type of Writing					Idea for Performance Task
			Drawing	Graphic Organizer	Sentence	Paragraph N	Paragraph E	Multi-Paragraph N	Multi-Paragraph E	
N	Jackie Robinson	IU List		GO15			X			What were the three most important events in the life of Jackie Robinson?
		DI Explain		GO15 GO41					X	Why should Jackie Robinson be thought of as a great person and a great baseball player?
		MC Explain		GO33 GO31 GO36				X		Pretend that you are Jackie Robinson and write a story telling what you did and how you felt.
		CS Evaluate DI Explain		GO38 GO39 GO41					X	Did this book help you in your research about great Americans?
O	Owl Moon	IU Describe		GO14						List the words that describe what it would be like to be in the forest owling.
		DU Explain		GO6					X	Teach someone how to go owling. How would you do it?
		MC Explain		GO14 GO41			X			From your research about owls, what is an owl like?
		CS Judge		GO11			X			Did the author do a good job of showing that the child was brave? How?

Level	Book Title	Thinking Skill Verb	Drawing	Graphic Organizer	Sentence	Paragraph N	Paragraph E	Multi-Paragraph N	Multi-Paragraph E	Idea for Performance Task
P	Find The Titanic	IU Illustrate & Label	X							What did the Titanic look like at the bottom of the ocean?
		DI Explain		GO14 GO31 GO32 GO37				X		Tell a true story about what it was like to explore the Titanic at the bottom of the ocean.
		MC Compare		GO18 GO31 GO32 GO36				X		It was exciting to find the lost Titanic. What have you lost that you were excited to find?
		CS Rate		GO39					X	Did this book give you good information about the Titanic? What?
P	The Search For The Missing Bones	DI Illustrate & Label								Draw a picture of a bone from your arm or leg and label the parts.
		DI Categorize		GO12			X			What are two categories that could be used for bones?
		MC Generalize		GO40 GO39 GO41					X	From your research about the human skeleton, what is the function of the skeleton?
		CS Evaluate		GO27			X			This book combines a story with facts about the human skeleton. Is this a good way to teach us about bones? Why?

Creating the Performance Tasks from the Ideas

Figure 2.10 shows four ideas for performance tasks for each of the leveled books in the continuum. Except for one task for the book, *Jackie Robinson*, each task uses one of the thinking-skill verbs. Although four performance tasks are available for each of these books, the teacher may only choose to use one or two. The ideas for seven of these books have been developed into performance tasks and are included in this chapter. Figure 2.11 correlates these books with their levels and with the performance tasks and assessment lists found in Chapter 3.

Figure 2.11. Seven Books: Their Levels and Performance Tasks and Assessments

Book	Level	Figures (found in Chapter 3)
Happy Birthday	C	3.16 through 3.19
Sid and Sam	E	3.20 through 3.23
Firefighters	G	3.24 through 3.27
Peeping and Sleeping	I	3.28 through 3.31
Amanda Pig and Her Big Brother Oliver	K	3.32 through 3.35
A Chair for My Mother	M	3.36 through 3.43
Jackie Robinson	N	3.44 through 3.52

The following are comments on these performance tasks.

Performance Tasks for *Sid and Sam* (found in Chapter 3)

- These two tasks ask for the student to put words and phrases into graphic organizers.
- The Initial Understanding task asks for literal understanding.
- The Developing an Understanding task asks for a higher-order interpretation.
- The audiences used in these tasks include the reading teacher, the music teacher, a friend, and the school librarian. The student work can actually be given to this audience. Creating audiences enhances

motivation and helps the student learn to "communicate" with different audiences.

♦ Again, the Procedure is a simple list of what to do and it stresses the use of the assessment lists.

♦ These performance tasks are short.

Performance Tasks for *Firefighters* (found in Chapter 3)

♦ This is a nonfiction book.

♦ A field trip to a firehouse might be a good introductory activity.

♦ The first task asks for a graphic organizer and a sentence.

♦ The second task for this book comprise a "set" of tasks. The first two tasks are needed for work on the third task. The first two tasks are "research" to support the work on the third task. The fourth task asks the student to evaluate the quality of the book *Firefighters* as an information source.

♦ This set of performance tasks does not include tasks for Initial Understanding and Developing an Interpretation. A problem to avoid is having too many Initial Understanding tasks and too few Critical Stance tasks.

♦ The Making Connections tasks ask the student to use the information from the first two tasks to draw a picture of a firefighter at work and write a sentence about what a firefighter does.

♦ The audience for the drawing and sentence is the firefighters. They can be sent to the firefighters visited during the field trip.

♦ This task provides an excellent opportunity for collaboration with the art teacher.

♦ Again, the Procedure simply outlines the steps to take and the assessment lists will provide more details about what to do and how the quality of the work will be assessed.

Performance Tasks for *Happy Birthday* (found in Chapter 3)

♦ These two tasks call for drawings as the final product.

♦ See Chapters 4 and 5 in the first volume of this two-set series, *Assessing and Teaching Reading Comprehension and Pre-Writing, K–3,* for information about performance tasks and scoring tools for drawings.

♦ The task for Making Connections asks the student to think about their own birthdays.

- An audience is identified for each task. The audiences for these tasks include classmates, a friend, parents, and the author, Tami Butler.
- Notice that the statement of Purpose describes the impact the student work is intended to have on the audience. (The statement of Purpose is not a statement of the lesson-plan purpose of this task.)
- Notice that the items under the Procedure part of each task simply list the steps of the task. The assessment lists provide specific details and address the quality of the work.
- The Procedure stresses the use of the assessment list.
- The tasks are short and to the point.
- The task is written "to the student" who will be using the performance task.

Performance Tasks for *Peeping and Sleeping* (found in Chapter 3)

- These two tasks ask for graphic organizers and sentences.
- Audiences for these tasks are the reading teacher, the classroom teacher, and parents.
- The Critical Stance tasks ask each student to rate the book as to how good the title is. The teacher then uses this data to make a graph.

Performance Tasks for *Amanda Pig and Her Big Brother Oliver* (found in Chapter 3)

- This set of tasks involves making the transition from sentences to paragraphs.
- The audiences include the student's reading group, the whole class, Kindergarten Buddies, and the guidance counselor.

Performance Tasks for *A Chair for My Mother* (found in Chapter 3)

- These tasks make the transition from paragraphs to multiparagraph writing.
- One task calls for a drawing, a graphic organizer, and a multiparagraph story.
- One task calls for two graphic organizers and a multiparagraph story. The first graphic organizer asks the student to find sensory descriptive vocabulary and the second graphic organizer helps the student plan the story, which will incorporate those sensory words.
- The level of complexity of tasks is increasing.

- The teacher chooses the task or tasks to use. When the teacher selects a more complex task with several steps, the teacher can plan how to use time over several days to complete it.
- The audiences are cooperative learning partners, the people in the school, and classmates during Author's Afternoon, and the school librarian.

Performance Tasks for *Jackie Robinson* (found in Chapter 3)

- This is a nonfiction book.
- These tasks are on the "complex" end of the continuum for performance tasks for the primary grades. These tasks provide a research experience for the students.
- Only students who are very experienced with multistep performance tasks should use this set of performance tasks.
- The Making Connections task asks the student to use graphic organizers to analyze Jackie Robinson, to create a setting, and to plan a story from the point of view of Jackie Robinson.
- The student is the audience for the Developing an Interpretation task because this task prepares the student for the Making Connections task—to write a story from the point of view of Jackie Robinson.
- The audience for the story from Jackie Robinson's point of view is the readers of "Sports Illustrated for Kids."
- The statement of Procedure is a checklist of steps in the task.
- The assessment lists provide more specific details about what to do in each step and how the quality of the work will be assessed.

Creating Assessment Lists for Performance Tasks That Require Writing

The following are some comments about how assessment lists were created for the performance tasks in Chapter 3.

Assessment Lists for *Happy Birthday*

- Assessment items are written as questions the students would ask themselves.
- The assessment list items are very specific to the drawing asked for. Volume one in this two-set series, *Assessing and Teaching Reading Comprehension and Pre-Writing, K–3,* presents assessment tools for drawings.

- These assessment lists have three or four elements each. If there are too many items for some or all of the students in the class, then remove some of the items from the list. Do not remove the questions that relate to the content focus of the performance task.
- The assessment list is designed to help students pay attention to as much as the teacher can get them to pay attention to.
- An item such as, "Does my picture show how I know that Duck and Pig are friends?" is a "Sure Thing" item because it will be easy for students to use. Assessment lists should contain "Sure Thing" items.
- An item such as, "Did I use details in my picture?" may be a stretch for students until they have had experiences to learn about what it means to have the right amount of detail in a drawing. An assessment list should contain only one "Challenge" item.

Assessment Lists for *Sid and Sam*

- Assessment items are written as questions the students would ask themselves.
- The assessment list items are very specific to the graphic organizer asked for.
- Assessment lists include items like, "Did I write my name on my graphic organizer?" These are yes or no type items. These items also reinforce good work habits.
- Assessment lists include items like, "Did I leave space between my words?", which may call for some interpretation.
- Assessment lists include items that call for a quantity, such as, "Did I show three things that made Sid and Sam happy?"
- Assessment lists include asking about a number of elements in one item, such as, "Did I draw small pictures for beginning, middle, and ending?" This item is asking four questions: "Did I draw small pictures?" "Did I use my smart fingers to draw small pictures for the beginning?", "Did I draw small pictures for the middle?", and "Did I draw small pictures for the ending?" If these types of assessment list items are too complex for the students, then revise the assessment list to have items that focus on only one element at a time.

Assessment Lists for *Firefighters*

- Assessment items are written as questions the students would ask themselves.
- The assessment list items are very specific to the graphic organizer asked for. Volume one in this two-set series, *Assessing and Teaching*

Reading Comprehension and Pre-Writing, K–3, presents assessment tools for graphic organizers.

- The assessment lists for "What Do Firefighters Do?" is an assessment list for a sentence.

Assessment Lists for *Peeping and Sleeping*

- Assessment items are written as questions the students would ask themselves.

- Some items are very clear, such as, "Did I give a "Yes" or "No" rating to the title?" and are "Sure Thing" items. These are easy for the student to understand.

- Some items are more open-ended and require interpretation, such as, "Did I give one good reason for my opinion?" Classroom discussion would have had to take place about the difference between a reason and a good reason for this assessment list item to be meaningful to the student. The teacher needs to study the assessment lists well before the task is used with students, then plan which assessment list items must be the subject of classroom work before the performance task and assessment list are used.

Assessment Lists for *Amanda Pig and Her Big Brother Oliver*

- Assessment items are written as questions the students would ask themselves.

- An example of an assessment list item that would require preliminary classroom work is, "Did I write a clear main idea?" This item is asking the student to know what a main idea is and to understand the difference between a clear main idea and an unclear main idea. The students would need to have classroom discussions on this topic and see examples of writing with no main idea, writing with an unclear but present main idea, and writing with a clear main idea.

- One assessment list has the item, "Did I use at least two supporting details?" Here the teacher may ask the student to underline each of the two supporting details. This tells the teacher if the student can identify the supporting details that he used.

Assessment Lists for *A Chair for My Mother*

- Assessment items are written as questions the students would ask themselves.

- One assessment list item asks, "Did I draw a picture of what the mother would buy next?" Here the response is a "yes" or "no."

- Another assessment list item asks, "Did I list some interesting actions?" The word "interesting" makes this assessment list item more challenging. Classroom discussions about what makes actions interesting to the reader help the student learn how to use assessment list items like this.

- Again, items like, "Is my ending interesting?" and "Did I use many descriptive words?" work on the assessment list only if the student has had enough prior experience with what these items mean.

- An item in one assessment list asks, "Did I use a variety of types of sentences in my story?" works if the student knows how to use and identify simple, compound, and complex sentences. The teacher may ask the student to label each sentence as to what type of sentence it is.

Assessment Lists for *Jackie Robinson*

- Assessment items are written as questions the students would ask themselves.

- Performance tasks for this book ask students to write multi-paragraph narrative stories and expository pieces. A short assessment list cannot focus on all the elements of multiparagraph writing. Each assessment list should focus on some aspect of multiparagraph writing to which the students should pay particular attention.

- A particular assessment list for expository writing may focus on main idea, supporting details, and conclusion. Another assessment list for expository writing may focus on the use of descriptive language, sentence variety, and punctuation. Assessment lists should be created to reinforce what students already do well (sure thing items) and challenge them to improve their performance (challenge items.)

- When performance tasks have several steps before the final written product is started, the teacher should stop the students after each step and have them assess their work. The teacher also assesses the work, and the students make improvements before they move on to the next step in the task.

- When the first draft of the written product, such as a story or essay, is completed, the students assess their own work and the teacher assesses it also. The students can use this feedback to revise the writing and then assess it again using the same assessment list. Here the students are beginning to go through a more complete writing process.

Ideas for Assessment List Items

(The menus of ideas for items for assessment lists are found in Chapter 3.)

Figures 3.12 through 3.15 provide menus of ideas for assessment lists. Some of these items may be used as they are presented here and some should be revised to be more specific to the particular performance task. These ideas for assessment list items were derived from the details of the highest levels of performance described in the analytic rubrics for writing.

Performance Tasks and Assessment Lists Are Learning Activities as Well as Opportunities for Assessment

Each performance task is a learning activity. Students are asked to use information from what they have read and experienced. They process it in a graphic organizer according to the thinking-skill verb and present a final performance or product. The act of constructing the response is an act of learning. Because many of the tasks use higher-order thinking-skill verbs, many of the tasks result in higher-order learning.

The assessment list is a tool constructed to focus the student's attention on some particular aspect of this construction process so that components of the process will improve. The teacher creates the assessment list to reinforce what the students can already do and to improve their performance in some important way.

The teacher anticipates the performance task or tasks that will be used for a particular book, and studies the performance task, graphic organizers used for it, and it's assessment list. The teacher may decide to use those materials "as is" or to modify them to better meet the needs of the students.

Once the teacher is set with the performance task, graphic organizer(s), and assessment list, the teacher develops lesson plans to teach students what they will need to know to be successful on the performance task. For example, the teacher may need to help the students understand how to use a particular type of graphic organizer better. The students may need to see and talk about examples of writing with clear main ideas with three supporting details. They may need to see examples of flawed work to understand how to have clear main ideas and sufficient supporting details in their own writing. The performance tasks and their graphic organizers and assessment lists help the teacher focus instruction.

The first criterion to judge the quality of a performance task and its supporting materials is, "**This is a great learning activity that is worth the time it takes!**" Once that criterion has been met, then the performance task can also be used as an opportunity to assess the degree to which the students understand what they have read. The performance task also assesses the degree to which the student has mastered information organization and writing skills.

Making Adaptations for Students at Risk

The classroom teacher, other educators, and support staff can make adaptations to the materials and how they are used with students. Some suggestions for these adaptations include:

- Form small, temporary groups of students who need help learning how to use a graphic organizer. Work directly with them to model how to use the graphic organizer. Share the work of putting information into the graphic organizer. Show them "terrific" work on graphic organizers and ones that "need work" and then help them improve the one that needs work until it is terrific.

- Form small temporary groups of students who need help learning how to "see" the way quality is being defined. For example, what does it mean when the assessment list item asks for "clear" main ideas, or "sufficient" details, or "neat" work?

- If some students are struggling with a graphic organizer, do not give them tasks that ask for work on a graphic organizer *and* a written product. When these students become comfortable with using a graphic organizer, the performance tasks can be extended to include a written product.

- Modify the assessment list when absolutely necessary. The assessment list used by most students may have four items. An adapted assessment list may have only two items. Another assessment list used by most students may have an item that says, "Did I give three details?" and the adapted assessment list item reads, "Did I give two details?"

- Although the graphic organizer and/or the assessment list may be modified sometimes, the performance task usually does not need to be modified.

- It is important to allow all students to work with the same thinking-skill verbs. Teachers should not engage most students with a task asking for an inference and ask the students "at risk" to only make a list. Care must be taken not to focus on Initial Understanding with students at risk to the exclusion of the other three levels of thinking.

- Coach students to be more accurate self-assessors. Sit with a student and focus on one item on the assessment list and the student's work that is relevant to that one item. Gently help the students focus on their work and talk about how it does or does not meet the standards.

Glossary

Benchmarks

A benchmark is a piece of student writing (or drawings and graphic organizers) that has been selected to define a specific level of quality. A benchmark for work at the **Beginning** level shows what student performance looks like at the early stages of writing. Benchmarks at the **Developing, Consolidating**, and **Extending** levels show what student performance looks like as they progress along the writing continuum.

The titles for these four levels of writing were taken from the series by the Education Department of Western Australia: *First Steps Writing Resource Book* (1994). Portsmouth, NH: Heinemann. This book, and others from First Steps, provide actual samples of student work for each of these benchmarks.

Benchmarks are primarily used for three purposes. First, the teacher selects an appropriate benchmark to use as a model to show students so that they can see a level of quality towards which to aspire. The teacher takes care to select a benchmark that is just enough of a stretch to inspire improvement without discouraging students. Teachers can show one benchmark to some students and a different benchmark to other students so that all students have an appropriate goal.

The second reason to use benchmarks is to help the teacher place a student's writing in a continuum of writing performance. Once the writing is placed, the teacher can focus instruction and materials to help the student work towards the next level of performance.

The third reason to use the benchmarks is to help parents understand where their child stands in the continuum of performance for the grade level. In the primary grades the emphasis is movement along a continuum of development.

First-Draft Writing

First-draft writing is what students do when they write without revising. The student may have made a drawing and/or completed a graphic organizer in the pre-writing steps, but the student completed only one draft of the writing.

Final-Draft Writing

Final draft writing is writing that shows what students can do when they get feedback on the first draft. The student then improves the work to a final version. This feedback comes through self-assessment and assessment from the teacher and others.

Independent Writing

Independent writing is what students do when they are writing by themselves.

Interactive Writing

Interactive writing is where the teacher and the students write together. This can occur in a whole-class group or in smaller groups. The writing may be done on a chalk or white board, on a flip chart, or with the use of an overhead projector. The process includes the following:

- ♦ The teacher engages the students in a reading activity that could be a Read-Aloud, Shared Reading, or Guided Reading.
- ♦ The teacher defines the writing assignment with an **emphasis on the thinking-skill verb** most important to the writing task.
- ♦ The teacher introduces a **graphic organizer** and works with the students to put information into it. A large-size graphic organizer is presented on an easel so that students and the teacher can take turns writing. The teacher and students discuss the information that is put into the graphic organizer.
- ♦ The teacher works with the students to write a first draft.
- ♦ The teacher and students talk about word choice and may make some revisions.
- ♦ The teacher and students assess the writing using an assessment list.

The teacher may introduce an independent writing assignment by modeling through "Interactive Writing." The writing tasks used for interactive writing and independent writing would have the same thinking-skill verb and graphic organizer.

Level of Performance

A level of performance is a specific level of quality of a specific type of student work. For example, a piece of student work is selected to represent a specific level of quality of student writing. This piece of student writing is called a benchmark for that level of quality.

In this chapter, four levels of performance for student writing are used. Each level would have its own benchmark, e.g., sample of student work to represent it. Each of these four levels of quality has a name and they are as follows:

- ♦ **Extending** as a writer = highest level in this continuum
- ♦ **Consolidating** as a writer
- ♦ **Developing** as a writer
- ♦ **Beginning** as a writer = lowest level in this continuum

Student Dictionary

A student dictionary (*Words I Use When I Write*, by Trisler and Howe. Rosemount, NJ: Modern Learning Press). is a consumable booklet of high-frequency words, word families, and blank spaces where students may add their own words to support the development of spelling and vocabulary in the context of their reading and writing. Each student has a Student Dictionary to which they may refer and add to during the year. Student dictionaries support student writing.

Types of Writing

♦ **Expository Writing**: This is writing to explain, teach, or inform the audience about the story or the information in nonfiction text. Sometimes Expository writing is called Informative writing. Expository writing is the most common kind of writing in performance tasks because students are asked to do things such as sequence, describe, predict, and compare. Students can respond to both fiction and non-fiction through expository writing.

♦ **Narrative Writing**: This is the storytelling form of writing usually written in the first person "I," to tell a story with a beginning, middle and ending. Primary-grade students may begin narrative writing by writing a sentence about what they did. Later the students work up to writing paragraphs and stories. Journal writing is another opportunity for narrative writing. A purpose of narrative writing is to entertain the audience.

Students can respond to fiction through using narrative writing to continue the story, i.e., "Write a story that would show what would come next." Students can also create new stories that connect text to text, i.e., "Write a story that shows what would happen if Max in *Where the Wild Things Are* met the Wolf in *The Three Little Pigs*." Students can also create stories that connect themselves to what they read, i.e., "Write a story that shows what would happen if you and Little Bear were friends."

Students can also respond to nonfiction through narrative writing. A child can write a narrative story about living in the desert, or making maple syrup in a small New England town, or exploring the world in search of new spiders. Accurate facts from their studies of those topics form the information foundation for a story with a beginning, middle, and end.

♦ **Persuasive Writing**: This writing is intended to persuade the audience of a particular point of view or course of action to take. It is clearly "persuasive" in tone and actually asks the audience to agree with the author's point of view. Persuasive writing is rare in the early grades. Persuasive conversation is more common. Some Critical Stance performance tasks allow students opportunities to engage in persuasive writing. Here, students are asked to judge, rate, evaluate, and present the evidence for their opinion. They are attempting to persuade the audience of their point of view.

This book does not include performance tasks or assessment tools for persuasive writing. They will be left for the later grades.

Word Wall

A word wall begins with an alphabet posted along the top of a wall. Students names are the first words added, followed by high-frequency words such as "and, I, my, me, the, and was." Students should be able to spell the words on the Word Wall. When the students have learned to spell the posted high-frequency words, they are removed and other high-frequency words are added. Word walls support student writing.

Word Web in Centers

Word Webs in centers are collections of vocabulary words relevant to the topic in a particular center. If there are three centers operating in the classroom, each would have its own Word Web. Words are added as the class learns more about the topics in the centers. Word Webs also support student writing.

Writing Centers

These are centers set up for writing assignments relevant to literature, social social studies, science, or other weekly lessons. Books, benchmarks, word webs and other materials are located there. After they have been discussed in a group setting, performance tasks can be used in writing centers.

3

Assessment Tools and Performance Tasks for Writing

Topics in This Chapter

- A collection of graphic organizers for pre-writing as described in Chapter 2.
- A collection of assessment tools for writing as described in Chapter 2.
- A collection of performance tasks for leveled books as described in Chapter 2.

Graphic Organizers for Pre-Writing

Graphic Organizers GO1 through GO29 are found in the first volume of this two-set series, *Assessing and Teaching Reading Comprehension and Pre-Writing, K–3*. These graphic organizers help the student structure information processing such as sequencing, inferring, predicting, comparing, contrasting, evaluating, and judging. These graphic organizers are used for both fiction and nonfiction.

Graphic Organizers GO30 through GO43 as shown in this chapter, help the student organize information so that it may be incorporated into a final, written product, such as a sentence, a paragraph, or a multiparagraph piece. The writing can be either fiction or nonfiction. Figure 3.1 correlates assessment tools with corresponding figures in this chapter; Figure 3.2 matches a menu of ideas for assessment lists with corresponding figures in this chapters; and Figure 3.3 correlates performance tasks for leveled books with the corresponding figures in this chapter.

Figure 3.1. Assessment Tools for Writing

Assessment Tool For	Found in Figure:
Analytic Rubric for a Narrative Paragraph	3.4
Analytic Rubric for an Expository Paragraph	3.5
Holistic Rubric for a Narrative Paragraph	3.6
Holistic Rubric for an Expository Paragraph	3.7
Analytic Rubric for a Multiparagraph Story	3.8
Analytic Rubric for a Multiparagraph Expository Piece	3.9
Holistic Rubric for a Multiparagraph Story	3.10
Holistic Rubric for a Multiparagraph Expository Piece	3.11

Figure 3.2. Menu of Ideas for Items for Assessment Lists

Menu of Ideas for Assessment Lists for A	Found in Figure:
Narrative Paragraph	3.12
Expository Paragraph	3.13
Multiparagraph Story	3.14
Multiparagraph Expository Piece	3.15

Figure 3.3. Performance Tasks for Leveled Books

Level	Book Title	Performance Tasks See Figures:
C	*Happy Birthday*, by Tami Butler, illustrated by Pam Paparone	3.16 through 3.19
E	*Sid and Sam*, by Nola Buck, pictures by G. Brian Karas	3.20 through 3.23
G	*Firefighters*, by Norma Simon, illustrated by Pam Paparone	3.24 through 3.27
I	*Peeping and Sleeping*, by Fran Manushkin, illustrated by Jennifer Plecas	3.28 through 3.31
K	*Amanda Pig and Her Big Brother Oliver*, by Jean Van Leeuwen, pictures by Ann Schweninger	3.32 through 3.35
M	*A Chair for My Mother*, by Vera B. Williams	3.36 through 3.43
N	*Jackie Robinson*, by Jim O'Connor	3.44 through 3.52

Name: _____ Date: _____

Problem–Solution

The Problem   **The Solution**

_____   _____

_____   _____

_____   _____

_____   _____

_____   _____

_____   _____

_____   _____

_____   _____

GO30

Name: _____

Dare: _____

Draw The Setting Here

Write Descriptive Words About the Setting Below

I see:

I smell:

I hear:

I feel:

GO36

Name: _____ Date: _____

Draw the Main Character Here

Write words that describe the character...

Size:	Features:

Clothing:	Facial expression:

Unusual characteristics:

GO32

Name: _____ Date: _____

Character: _____

Being the Character

Answer as if you were the character.

I am proud of _____

_____

I am happy because _____

_____

I am unhappy because _____

_____

I am angry because _____

_____

I am curious about _____

_____

My strengths are _____

_____

My weaknesses are _____

_____

I would describe myself as _____

_____

Others would describe me as _____

_____

I want to get better at _____

_____

My goal in life is _____

_____

Overall, the words that describe me are: _____

_____

Name: _____ Date: _____

Story Map #1

Title:
Problem:

$$\downarrow$$

Action:

$$\downarrow$$

Conclusion:

GO34

Name: _____ Date: _____

Story Map #2

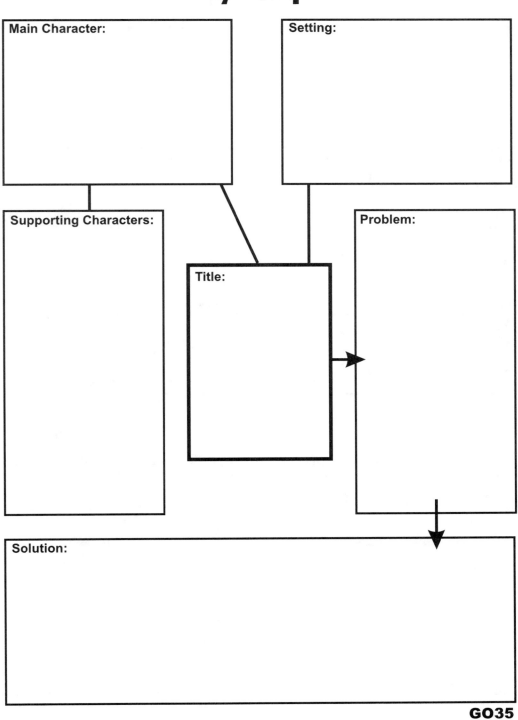

Main Character:

Setting:

Supporting Characters:

Title:

Problem:

Solution:

GO35

Name: _____ Date: _____

Story Map #3

Title:

Characters:

Setting: Time & Place:

Problem:

Event:

Event:

Event:

Solution:

GO36

Name: _____

Date: _____

Story Title: _____

Story Plan #4

Somebody (the character):

The character was trying to do something.
What was it?

But something got in the way?
What was it?

So, how did the character work it out?

GO37

Name: _____   Date: _____

QKWL Chart

What is my research Question?		
What do I Know?	What do I Want to know?	What did I Learn?

GO38

Name: _____ Date: _____

Evaluating Information Sources

Title: _____

Author (s): _____

Date Published: _____

Check one box for each item used in this evaluation. Add other items if necessary.

Item	Rating			
	YES!!	Yes	No	NO!!
Can I read this material?				
Is this information about my topic?				
Is this information up-to-date?				
Is the author qualified to write on this topic?				
Do the illustrations and/or photographs give me good information?				
Comments:				

GO39

Name: _____ Date: _____

Research Notes

My topic:		
My Questions	*Answers I Found*	*Sources of This Information*

GO40

Name: _____ Date: _____

Expository Writing Organizer #1

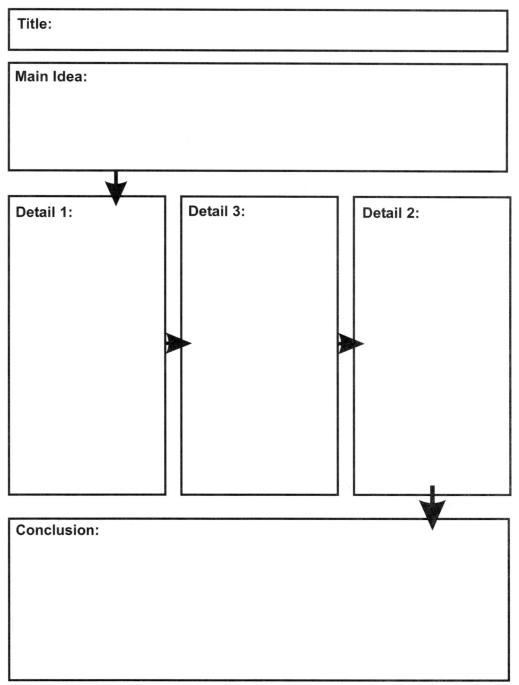

Title:

Main Idea:

Detail 1:

Detail 3:

Detail 2:

Conclusion:

GO41

Name: _____ Date: _____

Expository Writing Organizer #2

Topic:		
Part	**Notes**	**Vocabulary to Use**
Main Idea		
Detail #1		
Detail #2		
Detail#3		
Ending		

GO42

Name: _____ Date: _____

Expository Writing Organizer #3

Essential Qustion:

Answers I found that will help me answer the essential question:	Where I found this answer:

GO43

Figure 3.4. Analytic Rubric for a Narrative Paragraph

Trait of Writing	Levels of Quality			
	Extending	**Consolidating**	**Developing**	**Beginning**
Problem and Solution	A very interesting problem is presented and the solution is equally interesting. There may be an unexpected twist in the solution. The title of the story is well suited to the story and is interesting.	An interesting problem is presented and the solution is equally interesting. The title of the story is well suited to the story.	The problem maybe somewhat unclear. The solution may be abrupt or too obvious. The title is not well suited to the theme.	No clear problem is presented. The title may be missing.
Character	Well developed.	Developed.	Poorly developed.	Not developed.
Setting	Well-developed.	Developed.	Poorly developed.	Not developed.
Supporting Details	Three accurate supporting details are used.	Two accurate supporting details are used.	One accurate supporting detail is used. Other details may be inaccurate and/or off-topic.	No supporting details are used or those that are used are off-topic and/or inaccurate.
Dialogue	Some dialogue is attempted and is effective in developing the character and/or theme or plot of the story.	Some dialogue is attempted but may not be effective, i.e., it seems "stuck into" the story.	Dialogue is not attempted.	Dialogue is not attempted.

Organiza-tion	The paragraph has a beginning sentence, which is usually the main idea. Supporting details are presented in a logical and interesting order in the next sentences. The paragraph ends with a concluding sentence.	The paragraph has a beginning sentence, which is usually the main idea. Supporting details are presented in a logical order in the next sentences.	The paragraph has a beginning sentence, which is usually the main idea. Supporting details are presented in the next sentences, but they may not be in any particular order.	The paragraph has no apparent organization.
Transi-tional Words	Several transitional words are used effectively to help the story read smoothly.	One to two transitional words are used effectively.	One transitional word is used effectively.	Transitional words are not used.
Sentence Structure	There is some variety of correct sentences and they add interest to the story.	Sentences are complete but they are all the same.	Some sentences are incorrect.	Several sentences are incorrect.
Focus	All of the writing is very focused on the topic.	All of the writing is on the topic.	Most of the writing is on the topic.	Most or all of the writing is off-topic.
Vocabu-lary	The student has chosen vocabulary that is relevant to the content of the topic. Especially interesting describing words related to the various senses have also been chosen.	The student has chosen some vocabulary words that are relevant to the content of the topic. Accurate describing words related to some senses have also been chosen.	The student has chosen a small number of words from the vocabulary lists for this topic. Only a few describing words are used.	The student has not chosen words specific to the topic. Describing words are also lacking.
Language Mechanics and Spelling	Completely correct.	A few minor errors may be present but the work is still easy to read.	A number of errors make the work difficult to read.	There are so many errors that the work is very difficult to read.
Neatness	Very neat and easy to read.	Neat and easy to read.	The writing is somewhat difficult to read because of lack of neatness.	The writing is very difficult to read because of lack of neatness.

Figure 3.5. Analytic Rubric for an Expository Paragraph

Trait of Writing	*Levels of Quality*			
	Extending	Consolidating	Developing	Beginning
Main Idea	The main idea is very clear and very focused on the topic of the assignment. The title is very well suited to the main idea.	The main idea is clear and accurate according to the topic. The title is well suited to the main idea.	The main idea is there, but may be somewhat unclear. The title is somewhat suited to the main idea.	There is no main idea. The title may be absent.
Sup-porting Details	Three accurate supporting details are used.	Two accurate supporting details are used.	One accurate supporting detail is used. Other details may be inaccu-rate and/or off-topic.	No supporting details are used or those that are used are off-topic and/or inaccurate.
Organiza-tion	The paragraph has a beginning sentence, which is usually the main idea. Supporting de-tails are pre-sented in a logi-cal and interest-ing order in the next sentences. The paragraph ends with a con-cluding sen-tence.	The paragraph has a beginning sentence, which is usually the main idea. Supporting de-tails are pre-sented in a logi-cal order in the next sentences.	The paragraph has a beginning sentence, which is usually the main idea. Supporting de-tails are pre-sented in the next sentences, but they may not be in any partic-ular order.	The paragraph has no apparent organization.
Focus	All of the writing is very focused on the topic.	All of the writing is on the topic.	Most of the writing is on the topic.	Most or all of the writing is off-topic.
Transi-tional Words	Several transi-tional words are used effectively to help the writing read smoothly.	One to two tran-sitional words are used effectively.	One transitional word is used effectively.	Transitional words are not used.

Sentence Structure	There is a variety of correct sentences and they add interest to the writing.	Sentences are complete but they are all the same.	Some sentences are incorrect.	Several sentences are incorrect.
Vocabulary	The student has chosen vocabulary that is highly relevant to the content of the topic. Especially interesting describing words related to several senses have also been chosen.	The student has chosen some vocabulary words that are relevant to the content of the topic. Accurate describing words related to some senses have also been chosen.	The student has chosen a small number of words from the vocabulary lists for this topic. Only a few describing words are used.	The student has not chosen words specific to the topic. Describing words are also lacking.
Language Mechanics and Spelling	Completely correct.	A few minor errors may be present, but the work is still easy to read.	A number of errors make the work difficult to read.	There are so many errors that the work is very difficult to read.
Neatness	Very neat and easy to read.	Neat and easy to read.	The writing is somewhat difficult to read because of lack of neatness.	The writing is very difficult to read because of lack of neatness.

Figure 3.6. Holistic Rubric for a Narrative Paragraph

Level of Performance	Description of Writing at That Level of Quality
Extending	A clear and interesting problem is presented, and action leads to the solution. The solution or resolution may be unexpected and therefore more interesting. The title is very well suited to the problem–solution and catches the attention of the reader. One character is presented. A setting is established. The story is presented in a logical order. Transitional words are used effectively and a variety of correct sentences help the story read smoothly. All of the writing is on the topic. The student chose vivid vocabulary to develop the character, setting, and action. Language mechanics, spelling, and neatness are excellent. Overall, the paragraph is very interesting and engaging to the reader.
Consolidating	A clear and interesting problem is presented, and action leads to the solution. The setting is well suited to the problem–solution. One character is presented. A setting is established. The story is presented in a logical order. One or two transitional words are used effectively. There is no variety in sentence structure, although all sentences are correct. All of the writing is on the topic. The student chose vocabulary to develop the character, setting, and action. Any minor errors in language mechanics, spelling, or lack of neatness do not distract the reader.
Developing	A problem is presented and action leads to the solution. The title is somewhat related to the problem–solution. A character and setting may be mentioned but not developed. The story is presented in a logical order but some of the writing may be somewhat "off topic." Dialogue is not attempted. One transitional word is used effectively. There is no variety in sentence structure and some sentences are not complete. The vocabulary used to develop the character, setting, and action is not very vivid. Errors in language mechanics, spelling, or neatness distract the reader.
Beginning	The story lacks a clear problem. The writing rambles and the story line is lacking. Dialogue is not attempted. No transitional words are used. There is no variety in sentence structure, and several sentences are not complete. There are so many errors in language mechanics, and the work is so messy, that the work is extremely difficult to read, or cannot be read.

Figure 3.7. Holistic Rubric for an Expository Paragraph

Level of Performance	Description of Writing at That Level of Quality
Extending	The paragraph has a clear main idea that is very focused on the topic of the assignment. The title is very well suited to the main idea. Three accurate supporting details are presented in a logical order. All of the writing is on the topic. Several transitional words and a variety of correct sentences help the writing flow smoothly. The student chose vocabulary words that are very specific to the topic and also chose interesting describing words. Language mechanics, spelling, and neatness are excellent. Overall, the paragraph is very interesting and engaging to the reader.
Consolidating	The paragraph has a clear main idea focused on the topic of the assignment. The title is well suited to the main idea. Two accurate supporting details are included. All of the writing is on the topic. A few transitional words and a few correct sentences help the writing flow smoothly. The student chose vocabulary very specific to the topic and also used describing words accurately. Any minor errors in language mechanics, spelling, or lack of neatness do not distract the reader.
Developing	The paragraph has a main idea on the topic of the assignment, but it may lack clarity. The title is somewhat related to the main idea. One accurate supporting detail is included. Most of the writing is on the topic. Two accurate supporting details are included. All of the writing is on the topic. One transitional word is used. There is no sentence variety and some sentences may be incomplete. No vocabulary specifically related to the content of the topic has been used. Describing words may also be lacking. Errors in language mechanics, spelling, or neatness distract the reader.
Beginning	The paragraph lacks a main idea and is off-topic. The writing rambles. Transitional words are not used. Some sentences are incomplete. There are so many errors in language mechanics, and the work is so messy, that it is extremely difficult to read.

Figure 3.8. Analytic Rubric for
Multiparagraph Narrative Writing (Stories)

Trait of Writing	Levels of Quality			
	Extending	Consolidating	Developing	Beginning
Problem and Solution	A very interesting problem is presented and the solution is equally interesting. There may be an unexpected twist in the solution. The title of the story is well suited to the problem–solution and interesting to the reader.	An interesting problem is presented and the solution is equally interesting. The title of the story is well suited to the story.	The problem maybe somewhat unclear. The solution may be abrupt or too obvious. The title is somewhat well suited to the theme.	No clear problem is presented. The title may be missing.
Supporting Details	Many interesting and accurate supporting details add richness to the story.	Enough accurate supporting details are used to provide some substance to the story.	Only a few supporting details are used.	Very few supporting details are used.
Character	At least one interesting character is well developed.	One character is developed.	One character is presented but not well developed.	One character is presented but very poorly developed.
Setting	The setting is interesting and appropriate to the theme.	The setting is appropriate to the theme.	The setting is only slightly presented.	The setting is not presented.
Dialogue	Dialogue is used effectively to develop the character and/or develop the theme and action of the story.	Dialogue is attempted with modest success to present the character and/or theme and action of the story.	Dialogue is attempted, but with little success.	Dialogue is not attempted.

Sentence Variety	There is an effective variety of complete and correct sentences that make the story more interesting to read.	There is some variety of complete and correct sentences that make the story more interesting to read.	There is little variety in sentences. Some may be incomplete or incorrect.	There is no variety in sentence structure, and there are many mistakes in the sentences that are written.
Organization(Beginning, middle, and ending)	The story has a very clear beginning, middle, and end.	The story has a clear beginning, middle, and end.	There is not a clear structure of "beginning, middle, and end." One or more of these elements is weak.	There is a general lack of the structure, " beginning, middle, and end."
Transitional Words	The student uses a variety of transitional words very effectively to help make the story flow smoothly.	The student uses some transitional words to help improve the flow of the story.	The student uses very few transitional words and the story is choppy.	The student uses no transitional words and the story is very choppy.
Focus	The whole story is focused on the theme.	Most of the story is focused on the theme. Any deviation from the theme does not distract the reader.	The story deviates from the theme often enough to make the story difficult to follow.	The story lacks focus.
Vocabulary	Vivid vocabulary is very well chosen, appeals to many senses, and makes the story very interesting.	Vocabulary is well chosen, appeals to some senses, and makes the story interesting.	Vocabulary is bland and lacking in describing words.	The vocabulary is very poor.
Language Mechanics and Spelling	Completely accurate.	Minor errors do not distract the reader.	There are enough errors that the reader is distracted.	There are so many errors that the story is very difficult to read.
Neatness	Very neat.	Neat.	Somewhat neat.	Not neat.

Figure 3.9. Analytic Rubric for Multiparagraph Expository Writing

Trait of Writing	Levels of Quality			
	Extending	*Consolidating*	*Developing*	*Beginning*
Main Idea	The main idea is very clear and on the topic of the assignment. The title is very well suited to the main idea.	The main idea is clear and on the topic of the assignment. The title is well suited to the main idea.	The main idea is there, but lacks clarity. The title is somewhat suited to the main idea.	The main idea is absent, off-topic, or very unclear. The title is absent or not well suited to the main idea.
Supporting Details	At least three details support the main idea. Each of these details is clearly explained.	At least two details support the main idea. Each of these details is explained.	One detail supports the main idea. It may not be explained fully or clearly.	If details are provided, they are not explained or they are inaccurate.
Organization (main idea, paragraphs supporting the main idea, conclusion)	The first paragraph presents the main idea, the next paragraph(s) presents and explains the supporting details. The supporting details are presented in a logical and interesting order. The last paragraph provides the conclusion.	The first paragraph presents the main idea, the next paragraph(s) presents and explains the supporting details. The last paragraph provides the conclusion.	The first paragraph presents the main idea, the next paragraph(s) presents and explains the supporting details. There may not be a clear conclusion.	There is no organization to the writing. It is a series of sentences and paragraphs that do not develop a main idea in a logical way.
Focus	The entire piece is tightly focused.	The entire piece is focused on the topic.	The writing is mostly focused on the topic.	The writing is off-topic or diverges from the topic often.

Sentence Variety	There is an effective variety of complete and correct sentences that makes the story more interesting to read.	There is some variety of complete and correct sentences that make the story more interesting to read.	There is little variety in sentences. Some may be incomplete or incorrect.	There is no variety in sentence structure, and there are many mistakes in the sentences that are written.
Transitional Words	The student uses a variety of transitional words very effectively to help make the story flow smoothly.	The student uses some transitional words to help improve the flow of the story.	The student uses very few transitional words and the story is choppy.	The student uses no transitional words and the story is very choppy.
Vocabulary	The student uses topic-specific words and many accurate and interesting describing words appealing to many senses.	The student uses topic-specific words and many accurate and interesting describing words appealing to several senses.	The student uses few topic-specific words with only a few describing words.	The student uses no topic-specific words and very few describing words.
Language Mechanics and Spelling	Completely correct.	Any minor errors do not distract the reader.	There are enough errors that the reader is distracted.	There are so many errors that the piece is very difficult to read.
Neatness	Very neat.	Neat.	Somewhat neat.	Not neat.

Figure 3.10. Holistic Rubric for
Multiparagraph Narrative Writing (Stories)

Level of Performance	Description of Writing at That Level of Quality
Extending	There is a clear and interesting problem followed by action that leads to an interesting solution or resolution. This resolution may take a twist that adds interest to the story. The title is very well suited to the problem–solution and catches the attention of the reader. The story has a clear and interesting beginning, middle, and ending. The setting and at least one character are well developed through the use of vivid vocabulary. Dialogue is used effectively to develop the character and/or the theme and plot of the story. A variety of transitional words and a variety of correct and complete sentences help make the story flow smoothly. All of the writing stays focused on the story. Mechanics and spelling are correct, and the work is very neat and presentable. Overall, the story is especially interesting.
Consolidating	There is a clear and interesting problem followed by action that leads to an interesting solution or resolution. The title is well suited to the problem–solution. The story has a clear beginning, middle, and ending. The setting and at least one character are developed through the use of vocabulary. Vivid vocabulary may be lacking. Dialogue is used to develop the character and/or the theme and plot of the story. Transitional words and some variety of correct and complete sentences help make the story flow smoothly. All of the writing stays focused on the story. Minor errors in mechanics and spelling do not distract the reader.
Developing	There is a problem followed by action that leads to a solution or resolution. The title is somewhat suited to the theme. There is some problem with the structure of "beginning, middle, and end" in this story. The character and/or the setting are poorly developed. Vivid vocabulary is clearly lacking. Dialogue is attempted to develop the character and/or the theme and plot of the story. Few transitional words are used, and there is little variety in sentence structure so the story is choppy. The writing may be off-topic in some places. Errors in mechanics and spelling distract the reader.
Beginning	A problem is not clearly presented. The title may be absent. There are significant problems with the structure of "beginning, middle, and end" in this story. The character and/or the setting are lacking or are very poorly developed. Vivid vocabulary is clearly lacking. Dialogue is not attempted. No transitional words are used, and there is no variety in sentence structure, so the story is very choppy. The writing is off-topic in some places. Errors in mechanics and spelling make the story very difficult to read.

Figure 3.11. Holistic Rubric for Multiparagraph Expository Writing

Level of Performance	Description of Writing at That Level of Quality
Extending	The main idea is accurate and clearly on the topic of the assignment. The title is very well suited to the main idea. Three accurate supporting details are presented and explained. The first paragraph presents the main idea. The next paragraph(s) present(s) the supporting details and there is a concluding paragraph. A variety of transitional words help make the writing smooth. All of the writing is on the topic. Vivid and content-specific vocabulary is used accurately. A variety of correct and complete sentences helps make the writing more interesting. Mechanics and spelling are correct. The work is very neat. Overall, the writing does an excellent job of teaching and explaining.
Consolidating	The main idea is accurate and on the topic of the assignment. The title is well suited to the main idea. Two accurate supporting details are presented and explained. The first paragraph presents the main idea. The next paragraph(s) present(s) the supporting details and there is a concluding paragraph. Some transitional words are used. All of the writing is on the topic. Content-specific vocabulary is used accurately. Some variety of complete and correct sentences are used. Minor errors in mechanics and spelling do not distract the reader. The work is neat.
Developing	The main idea is accurate and on the topic of the assignment. The title is somewhat suited to the main idea. One accurate supporting detail is presented and explained. The first paragraph presents the main idea. The next paragraph(s) presents the supporting details, but these may not be explained well. There is a concluding paragraph. Few transitional words are used and the writing is choppy. Some of the writing may be off-topic. Few content-specific words are used. There is little variation in sentence structure, and some sentences may be incomplete. Errors in mechanics and spelling distract the reader. The work is not neat.
Beginning	The main idea is not on the topic of the assignment. The title is absent or not well suited to the main idea. Supporting details are inaccurate or not provided. There is no apparent structure to the writing. No transitional words are used. Vocabulary is poorly used. There is no variety in sentence structure, and some sentences are incomplete. Major errors in mechanics and spelling make the work very difficult to read. The work is not neat.

Figure 3.12. Menu of Items for Assessment Lists for Narrative Paragraphs

Trait of Writing	Ideas for Items for Assessment Lists
Problem and Solution	Does my story tell about a problem? Do I tell about how the problem is solved? Is the problem interesting? Is the solution a good solution to the problem? Does the solution have an interesting twist?
Character	Does my story have a main character? Does my story "paint a picture" of the character? Is my character interesting?
Setting	Does my story have a setting? (where) Does my story have a setting? (when) Is the setting interesting? Does the setting help tell the story?
Supporting Details	Did I give details about the problem? Did I give details about the action in the story? Did I give details about the character? Did I give details about where the story took place? Did I give details about when the story took place?
Organization	Does my story have an interesting beginning? Does my story have action in the middle? Does my story have an interesting end? Does my story have a beginning, middle, and ending? Are the details in a sequential order to tell the story?
Transitional Words	Did I use transitional words from the list? Did I use words such as, and, also, then, next…?
Sentence Structure	Is each sentence a complete sentence?
Focus	Is my whole paragraph about the story?
Vocabulary	Did I use the words from the vocabulary list? Did I use words from my personal dictionary? Did I use descriptive words? Did I use words from the "Smell" list? Did I use words from the "See" list? Did I use words from the "Hear" list? Did I use words from the "Touch" list?
Language Mechanics & Spelling	Did I end the sentence with a punctuation mark? Did I use the period correctly? Did I use the question mark correctly? Did I use the exclamation point correctly? Are the high frequency words spelled correctly? Are the special vocabulary words spelled correctly?
Neatness	Is my work neat?

Figure 3.13. Menu Of Items For Assessment Lists For Expository Paragraphs

Trait of Writing	Ideas for Items for Assessment Lists
Main Idea	Do I have a main idea? Is my main idea on the topic? Is my main idea interesting?
Supporting Details	Do I have three (or some other number) supporting details? Are my supporting details on the topic? Are my supporting details accurate? Are my supporting details interesting?
Organization	Is my main idea at the beginning? Are the supporting details after the main idea? Is my conclusion last?
Focus	Is all of my writing on the topic?
Transitional Words	Did I use transitional words from the list? Did I use words such as, and, also, then, next...?
Sentence Structure	Is each sentence a complete sentence?
Vocabulary	Did I use the words from the vocabulary list? Did I use words from my personal dictionary? Did I use descriptive words? Did I use words from the "Smell" list? Did I use words from the "See" list? Did I use words from the "Hear" list? Did I use words from the "Touch" list?
Language Mechanics & Spelling	Did I end the sentence with a punctuation mark? Did I use the period correctly? Did I use the comma correctly? Did I use the question mark correctly? Did I use the exclamation point correctly? Are the high frequency words spelled correctly? Are the special vocabulary words spelled correctly?
Neatness	Is my work neat?

Figure 3.14. Menu Of Items For Assessment Lists For Multiparagraph Stories

Trait of Writing	Ideas for Items for Assessment Lists
Problem and Solution	Does my story tell about a problem? Do I tell about how the problem is solved? Is the problem interesting? Is the solution a good solution to the problem? Does the solution have an interesting twist?
Character	Does my story have a main character? Does my story "paint a picture" of the character? Is my character interesting? Does my story have other characters? Does my story "paint a picture" of the other characters?
Dialogue	Did I use dialogue? Does the dialogue help show the problem? Does the dialogue help show what happens? Does the dialogue help show the solution?
Setting	Does my story have a setting? (where) Does my story have a setting? (when) Is the setting interesting? Does the setting help tell the story?
Supporting Details	Did I give details about the problem? Did I give details about the action in the story? Did I give details about the main character? Did I give details about the other characters? Did I give details about where the story took place? Did I give details about when the story took place?
Organization	Does my story have an interesting beginning? Does my story have action in the middle? Does my story have an interesting ending? Does my story have a beginning, middle, and end? Are the details in a sequential order to tell the story? Does the action in the story have interesting complications?
Transitional Words	Did I use transitional words from the list? Did I use words such as, and, also, then, next…?
Sentence Structure	Is each sentence a complete thought? Is there variety in the types of sentences I used? Did I use simple and compound sentences? Did I use simple, compound, and complex sentences?
Focus	Is my whole paragraph about the story?

Vocabulary	Did I use the words from the vocabulary list? Did I use words from my personal dictionary? Did I use descriptive words? Did I use vivid descriptive words? Did I use powerful action words? Did I use words from the "Smell" list? Did I use words from the "See" list? Did I use words from the "Hear" list? Did I use words from the "Touch" list?
Language Mechanics & Spelling	Did I end the sentence with a punctuation mark? Did I use the period correctly? Did I use the comma correctly? Did I use quotation marks correctly? Did I use the question mark correctly? Did I use the exclamation point correctly? Are the high frequency words spelled correctly? Are the special vocabulary words spelled correctly?
Neatness	Is my work neat?

Figure 3.15. Menu Of Items For Assessment Lists For Expository Paragraphs

Trait of Writing	Ideas for Items for Assessment Lists
Main Idea	Do I have a main idea? Is my main idea on the topic? Is my main idea interesting?
Supporting Details	Do I have three (or some other number) supporting details? Are my supporting details on the topic? Are my supporting details accurate? Are my supporting details interesting?
Organization	Is my main idea at the beginning? Are the supporting details after the main idea? Are the supporting details in a sequential order? Is my conclusion last?
Focus	Is all of my writing on the topic?
Transitional Words	Did I use transitional words from the list? Did I use words such as, and, also, then, next…? Did I use words such as first, second, and third? Did I use the word "because" as a linking word? Did I use a variety of transitional words?
Sentence Structure	Is each sentence a complete sentence? Is there variety in the types of sentences I used? Did I use simple and compound sentences? Did I use simple, compound, and complex sentences?
Vocabulary	Did I use the words from the vocabulary list? Did I use words from my personal dictionary? Did I use descriptive words? Did I use vivid descriptive words? Did I use powerful action words? Did I use words from the "Smell" list? Did I use words from the "See" list? Did I use words from the "Hear" list? Did I use words from the "Touch" list?
Language Mechanics & Spelling	Did I end the sentence with a punctuation mark? Did I use the period correctly? Did I use the comma correctly? Did I use the question mark correctly? Did I use the exclamation point correctly? Are the high frequency words spelled correctly? Are the special vocabulary words spelled correctly?
Neatness	Is my work neat?

Figure 3.16a. Performance Task: Are Duck and Pig Friends?
see the assessment list on page 90

Background
The story shows that Duck and Pig both had birthdays. Were Duck and Pig friends? How do you know?

Task
Draw a picture that shows how you know that Duck and Pig were friends.

Audience
You will show your picture to your friend.

Purpose
Your picture will help your friend be happy.

Procedure
1. Talk with your teacher about the assessment list.
2. Draw the picture of how you know that Duck and Pig are friends.
3. Use the assessment list to check your work.

Figure 3.17a. Performance Task: How Do You Have Fun at Your Birthday Party?
see the assessment list on page 91

Background
We saw Duck and Pig have fun at their birthday party. How do you have fun at your own birthday party?

Task
Draw a picture of your favorite part of your own birthday party.

Audience
You will give your picture to your parents.

Purpose
When your parents see your picture, they will know what you like to do at your own birthday party.

Procedure
1. Talk with your teacher about the assessment list.
2. Draw the picture to show how you like to have fun at your own birthday party.
3. Use the assessment list to check your work.

Figure 3.16b. Performance Task Assessment List: Are Duck and Pig Friends?

1. Does my picture show how I know that Duck and Pig are friends?

Terrific   OK   Needs Work

2. Did I use details in my picture?

Terrific   OK   Needs Work

3. Is my work neat?

Terrific   OK   Needs Work

Figure 3.17b. Performance Task Assessment List:
How Do You Have Fun at Your Birthday Party?

1. Did I draw a picture that shows how I like to have fun at my own birthday party?

Terrific   OK   Needs Work

2. Did I use at least four colors to make my picture interesting?

Terrific   OK   Needs Work

3. Did I use details in my drawing?

Terrific   OK   Needs Work

Figure 3.18a. Performance Task:
What Happens in the Story?
see the assessment list on page 93

Background
We finished reading *Sid and Sam*. What happened in the story?
Task
Use the graphic organizer to show the beginning, middle, and ending of the story.
Audience
You will show your graphic organizers to the Reading Teacher.
Purpose
The Reading Teacher will be impressed by your work.
Procedure
1. Talk with your teacher about the assessment list.
2. Put information into the graphic organizer GO7 (see volume 1).
3. Check your work with the assessment list.

Figure 3.19a. Performance Task:
What Made Sid and Sam Happy?
see the assessment list on page 94

Background
What made Sid and Sam happy? What did they do that they enjoyed so much?
Task
Put information into a graphic organizer.
Audience
You will give your graphic organizers to your Music Teacher.
Purpose
Your graphic organizers will show your Music Teacher what makes some people happy.
Procedure
1. Talk with your teacher about the assessment list.
2. Put information into the graphic organizer GO11 (see volume 1).
3. Check your work with the assessment list.

Figure 3.18b. Performance Task Assessment List: What Happens in the Story?

1. Did I write my name on my graphic organizer?

Terrific   OK   Needs Work

2. Did I draw small pictures for the beginning, middle, and ending?

Terrific   OK   Needs Work

3. Did I write some words for the beginning, middle, and ending?

Terrific   OK   Needs Work

4. Is my work neat?

Terrific   OK   Needs Work

Figure 3.19b. Performance Task Assessment List: What Made Sid and Sam Happy?

1. Did I write my name on my graphic organizer?

Terrific   OK   Needs Work

2. Did I show three things that made Sid and Sam happy?

Terrific   OK   Needs Work

3. Did I leave spaces between my words?

Terrific   OK   Needs Work

4. Is my work neat?

Terrific   OK   Needs Work

Figure 3.20a. Performance Task:
What Do Firefighters Do?
see the assessment list on page 96

Background
We have read about firefighters. Some firefighters visited our school in their fire truck. What do firefighters do that is important to us?

Task
Draw a picture that shows what firefighters do that is important.

Audience
You will send your drawings to the firefighters.

Purpose
The pictures will show the firefighters that you know how important they are. The firefighters will feel happy.

Procedure
1. Talk with your teacher about the assessment list.
2. Use your work in graphic organizers GO12 and GO14 (see volume 1) to give you ideas for your picture.
3. Draw the picture.
4. Check your work with the assessment list.

Figure 3.21a. Performance Task:
Firefighters Do Important Work
see the assessment list on page 97

Background
Did the author do a good job of showing that firefighters do important work?

Task
To evaluate the author.

Audience
You will send your evaluations to the firefighters who visited your school.

Purpose
The firefighters will learn that you think they are important.

Procedure
1. Talk with your teacher about the assessment list.
2. Put information into the graphic organizer GO27 (see volume 1).
3. Check your work with the assessment list.

Figure 3.20b. Performance Task Assessment List: What Do Firefighters Do?

1. Did I write my name on my drawing?

Terrific   OK   Needs Work

2. Did I draw a picture of what a fireman does that is important?

Terrific   OK   Needs Work

3. Did I draw details?

Terrific   OK   Needs Work

4. Did I use color to emphasize what is happening in my drawing?

Terrific   OK   Needs Work

5. Did I show foreground, middleground, and background?

Terrific   OK   Needs Work

Figure 3.21b. Performance Task Assessment List: Firefighters Do Important Work

1. Did I write my name on my graphic organizer?

Terrific   OK   Needs Work

2. Did I pick Yes or No?

Terrific   OK   Needs Work

3. Did I give at least one good reason for my opinion?

Terrific   OK   Needs Work

4. Did I write a conclusion?

Terrific   OK   Needs Work

Figure 3.22a. Performance Task:
What Is *Peeping and Sleeping* About?

see the assessment list on page 99

Background
We just finished reading the story *Peeping and Sleeping*. What is this story about?
Task
Complete the Who, When, and Where graphic organizer.
Audience
Give the graphic organizer to the Reading Teacher.
Purpose
The Reading Teacher will see how well you can read.
Procedure
1. Talk with your teacher about the assessment list.
2. Put information into the graphic organizer GO16 (see volume 1).
3. Check your work with the assessment list.

Figure 3.23a. Performance Task:
Is This a Good Title?

see the assessment list on page 100

Background
Some books have very good titles. The titles help us know what the book is about. Is the title, *Peeping and Sleeping*, a good title?
Task
Use the title-rating paper to rate the title.
Audience
You will give your rating to your teacher, and your teacher will work with the class to make a graph of your opinions.
Purpose
Your rating will help make the graph.
Procedure
1. Talk with your teacher about the assessment list.
2. Put information into the graphic organizer GO25 (see volume 1).
3. Check your work with the assessment list.

Figure 3.22b. Performance Task Assessment List: What Is *Peeping and Sleeping* About?

1. Did I write my name on my graphic organizer?

Terrific   OK   Needs Work

2. Did I write the story title in the long box?

Terrific   OK   Needs Work

3. Did I write the answers to who, where, and when?

Terrific   OK   Needs Work

4. Did I check my spelling?

Terrific   OK   Needs Work

Figure 3.23b. Performance Task Assessment List: Is This a Good Title?

1. Did I write my name on my graphic organizer?

Terrific   OK   Needs Work

2. Did I give a Yes or No rating to the title?

Terrific   OK   Needs Work

3. Did I give one good reason for my opinion?

Terrific   OK   Needs Work

4. Did I give an idea for a new title for this book?

Terrific   OK   Needs Work

Figure 3.24a. Performance Task:
Why Did Amanda Copy Oliver?

see the assessment list on page 102

Background
Amanda copied many things that Oliver did. Sometimes Oliver became angry with at Amanda for copying him. Why did Amanda copy Oliver so much?
Task
Explain why Amanda copied Oliver.
Audience
You will read your explanation to the class.
Purpose
The class will be interested in your ideas.
Procedure
1. Talk with your teacher about the assessment list.
2. Write your explanation.
3. Check your work with the assessment list.

Figure 3.25a. Performance Task:
Brothers and Sisters at Play

see the assessment list on page 103

Background
Jean Van Leeuwen, the author of *Amanda Pig and Her Big Brother Oliver*, told a story about how brothers and sisters play with each other. Did Jean Van Leeuwen show how brothers and sisters really play with each other?
Task
Evaluate the way Jean Van Leeuwen showed how brothers and sisters play with each other.
Audience
You will give your evaluation form to the guidance counselor.
Purpose
The guidance counselor wants to know if the book about Amanda and Oliver shows how brothers and sisters play with each other.
Procedure
1. Talk with your teacher about the assessment list.
2. Put information into the graphic organizer GO27 (see volume 1). (The teacher will give you the question for the question box.)
3. Check your work with the assessment list.

Figure 3.24b. Performance Task Assessment List: Why Did Amanda Copy Oliver?

1. Did I write my name on my paper?

Terrific   OK   Needs Work

2. Did I write a clear main idea?

Terrific   OK   Needs Work

3. Did I give at least two supporting details?

Terrific   OK   Needs Work

4. Did I begin each sentence with a capital letter?

Terrific   OK   Needs Work

Figure 3.25b. Performance Task Assessment List: Brothers and Sisters at Play

1. Did I write my name on my graphic organizer?

Terrific   OK   Needs Work

2. Did I write the question in the question box?

Terrific   OK   Needs Work

3. Did I make a decision Yes or No?

Terrific   OK   Needs Work

4. Did I give at least one reason for my Yes or No?

Terrific   OK   Needs Work

5. Did I write a conclusion?

Terrific   OK   Needs Work

Figure 3.26a. Performance Task: What Will the Mother Buy Next?

see the assessment lists on pages 105, 106, and 107

Background

In the story, *A Chair for My Mother*, the mother saved her money and bought a wonderful, beautiful, fat, soft armchair.

She spent all of the money she saved on that chair. Now she is saving more money. What will she buy next?

Task

Tell a story about what she will buy next.

Audience

Your pictures and stories will go on our bulletin board in the hall.

Purpose

Your stories will entertain the other students.

Procedure

1. Study the assessment lists for this task.
2. Draw a picture of what the mother will buy next.
3. Plan your story with graphic organizer GO34 (see volume 1).
4. Write the story.
5. Use the assessment lists to check your work.

Figure 3.27a. Performance Task: What You Would Buy?

see the assessment lists on pages 108, 109, and 110

Background

In the story, *A Chair for My Mother*, the mother bought a wonderful, beautiful, fat, soft armchair. What would you save your money to buy?

Task

Write a story about how you would save money and what you would buy with it.

Audience

You will read your story during our classroom Authors' Afternoon.

Purpose

The students will be interested in your story.

Procedure

1. Study the assessment lists used for this task.
2. Use the graphic organizer GO14 (see volume 1) to describe the details of what you would buy.
3. Use graphic organizer GO36 (see volume 1) to plan your story.
4. Write your story.
5. Check your work with the assessment lists.
6. Read your story during Authors' Afternoon.

Figure 3.26b. Performance Task Assessment List: What Will the Mother Buy Next? (Drawing)

1. Did I write my name on my drawing?

2. Did I draw a picture of what the mother would buy next?

3. Did I use color for emphasis?

4. Did I show details?

5. Did I use descriptive words to label my drawing?

Figure 3.26c. Performance Task Assessment List: What Will the Mother Buy Next? (Graphic Organizer)

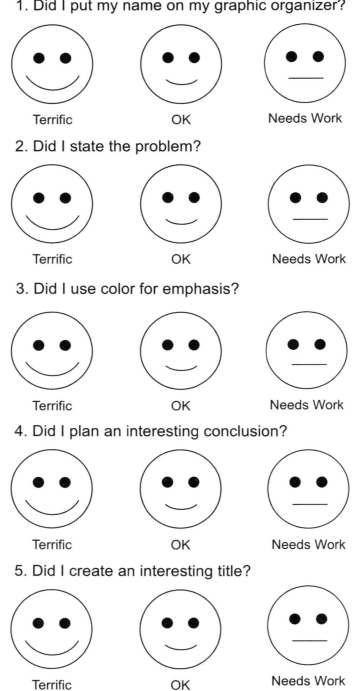

1. Did I put my name on my graphic organizer?

Terrific   OK   Needs Work

2. Did I state the problem?

Terrific   OK   Needs Work

3. Did I use color for emphasis?

Terrific   OK   Needs Work

4. Did I plan an interesting conclusion?

Terrific   OK   Needs Work

5. Did I create an interesting title?

Terrific   OK   Needs Work

Figure 3.26d. Performance Task Assessment List:
What Will the Mother Buy Next? (Story)

1. Does my story have an interesting beginning?

Terrific   OK   Needs Work

2. Does the action in my story have several details?

Terrific   OK   Needs Work

3. Is my ending interesting?

Terrific   OK   Needs Work

4. Did I use many descriptive words?

Terrific   OK   Needs Work

5. Are my words spelled correctly?

Terrific   OK   Needs Work

Figure 3.27b. Performance Task Assessment List: What You Would Buy? (Graphic Organizer GO14)

1. Did I write the name of what I would buy in the center oval?

Terrific   OK   Needs Work

2. Did I select at least three descriptive words for "I see"?

Terrific   OK   Needs Work

3. Did I select at least three descriptive words for "I hear"?

Terrific   OK   Needs Work

4. Did I select at least three descriptive words for "I smell"?

Terrific   OK   Needs Work

5. Did I select at least three descriptive words for "I feel"?

Terrific   OK   Needs Work

Figure 3.27c. Performance Task Assessment List: What You Would Buy? (Graphic Organizer GO36)

1. Did I plan the problem to be solved in my story?

Terrific   OK   Needs Work

2. Did I list three interesting actions for my story?

Terrific   OK   Needs Work

3. Did I plan an interesting conclusion?

Terrific   OK   Needs Work

4. Did I use describing words for at least two senses in my story?

Terrific   OK   Needs Work

5. Did I check my spelling?

Terrific   OK   Needs Work

Figure 3.27d. Performance Task Assessment List: What You Would Buy? (Story)

1. Does my story have an interesting title?

Terrific   OK   Needs Work

2. Does my story have a beginning, middle, and ending?

Terrific   OK   Needs Work

3. Did I use describing words for at least two senses?

Terrific   OK   Needs Work

4. Did I use a variety of types of sentences in my story?

Terrific   OK   Needs Work

5. Did I check my spelling?

Terrific   OK   Needs Work

Figure 3.28a. Performance Task:
How Great Was Jackie Robinson?

see the assessment lists on pages 112, 113, and 114

Background

Some people do not know who Jackie Robinson was. That is too bad because he was a great person and a famous baseball player.

Task

You job is to write an essay about the great Jackie Robinson.

Your essay will go on the school bulletin board titled "Great Americans."

Audience

Your audience are people who visit your school who do not know who Jackie Robinson was.

Purpose

You are trying to teach people that Jackie Robinson was a great American.

Procedure

1. Review the assessment lists for this task.
2. Complete graphic organizer GO15 (see volume 1).
3. Complete graphic organizer GO41 (see volume 1).
4. Write the essay.
5. Check your work with the assessment lists.

Figure 3.29a. Performance Task:
In Jackie Robinson's Shoes

see the assessment lists on pages 115, 116, 117, and 118

Background

What do you think it would be like to be Jackie Robinson and live a day in his life? Imagine that you could close your eyes, snap your fingers, and become the great Jackie Robinson for a day.

Task

Write a story about your experience as Jackie Robinson.

Audience

The audience for your story will be the readers of "Sports Illustrated."

Purpose

You want the readers to know and feel what Jackie Robinson experienced.

Procedure

1. Review the assessment lists for this task.
2. Complete graphic organizer GO33 (see volume 1). Your teacher will help you decide which parts to complete.
3. Complete graphic organizer GO31 (see volume 1) about the setting for your story.
4. Complete graphic organizer GO36 (see volume 1) to plan your story.
5. Write your story.
6. Check your work as you go with the graphic organizers.

Figure 3.28b. Performance Task Assessment List: How Great Was Jackie Robinson? (Fact Sheet)

1. Did I write what the facts were about in the box at the top?

2. Did I list three important facts about Jackie Robinson?

3. Is at least one fact about Jackie Robinson as a person?

4. Is at least one fact about Jackie Robinson as a baseball player?

Figure 3.28c. Performance Task Assessment List: How Great Was Jackie Robinson? (Expository Writing Organizer)

1. Did I write the main idea?

Terrific   OK   Needs Work

2. Did I list three details?

Terrific   OK   Needs Work

3. Are my details in an interesting order?

Terrific   OK   Needs Work

4. Did I write a memorable conclusion?

Terrific   OK   Needs Work

Figure 3.28d. Performance Task Assessment List: How Great Was Jackie Robinson? (Essay)

1. Do I have a clear main idea?

Terrific   OK   Needs Work

2. Did I use the three supporting details?

Terrific   OK   Needs Work

3. Did I explain why each detail was important?

Terrific   OK   Needs Work

4. Did I write a memorable conclusion?

Terrific   OK   Needs Work

5. Did I check my spelling?

Terrific   OK   Needs Work

Figure 3.29b. Performance Task Assessment List:
In Jackie Robinson's Shoes (Graphic Organizer GO33)

1. Did I write the name of the person I am studying at the top?

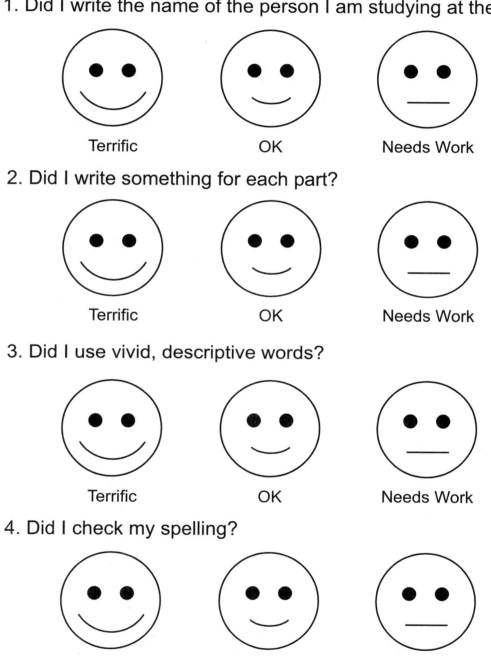

Terrific   OK   Needs Work

2. Did I write something for each part?

Terrific   OK   Needs Work

3. Did I use vivid, descriptive words?

Terrific   OK   Needs Work

4. Did I check my spelling?

Terrific   OK   Needs Work

Figure 3.29c. Performance Task Assessment List:
In Jackie Robinson's Shoes (Graphic Organizer GO31)

1. Did I draw a picture of the setting for my story about being Jackie Robinson for a day?

Terrific   OK   Needs Work

2. Did I show foreground, middleground, and background?

Terrific   OK   Needs Work

3. Did I use color to make the setting interesting?

Terrific   OK   Needs Work

4. Did I show details?

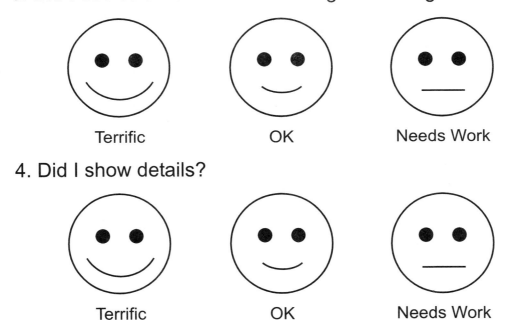

Terrific   OK   Needs Work

Figure 3.29d. Performance Task Assessment List: In Jackie Robinson's Shoes (Graphic Organizer GO36)

1. Did I create an interesting title for my story?

Terrific   OK   Needs Work

2. Did I state the problem that gets solved in my story?

Terrific   OK   Needs Work

3. Did I list three events that lead to a solution?

Terrific   OK   Needs Work

4. Did I state the way the problem would be solved by the end of my story?

Terrific   OK   Needs Work

Figure 3.29e. Performance Task Assessment List:
In Jackie Robinson's Shoes (Story)

1. Did I write about the problem in the beginning?

Terrific	OK	Needs Work

2. Did I write about some interesting action?

Terrific	OK	Needs Work

3. Did I present an interesting solution in my ending?

Terrific	OK	Needs Work

4. Did I use at least ten descriptive words from my graphic organizers?

Terrific	OK	Needs Work

4

Teaching and Assessing Reading Comprehension through Retelling

Topics in This Chapter

- Strategies to generate questions to engage students in retelling.
- Scoring tools for retelling.
- Strategies to use the questions and scoring tools for benchmark books.

Retelling Is a Strategy To Assess Comprehension

Running records are an assessment of text reading and provide a teacher with information different from isolated skill assessments. During a running record, a teacher will record a child's oral reading from a text, noting vocabulary, sentence pattern, pronunciation errors, and reading behaviors. The running record provides information that gives a teacher an accurate picture of how well a child is reading and helps to direct the teacher's instruction to support and guide the development of an individual student's reading strategies. (Clay, M. M. (2000). *Running records for classroom teachers*. Auckland, New Zealand: Heinemann.)

After a student reads the text, the teacher asks the child to retell the story in his own words. This retelling provides information about how well the student understood the text. When used together, running records and retelling can help the teacher determine the text difficulty and the individual reading progress of a student.

The purpose of this chapter is to provide strategies and tools to engage students in retelling and to assess their reading comprehension. Retelling can be used in conjunction with running records or it can be used anytime during, or after, any kind of reading activity, including read-alouds, shared reading, guided reading, or independent reading. Retelling can be used with individual students, leveled reading groups, literature circles, and whole-class discussions. In any of these contexts, the teacher asks the student(s) to "retell" the story in their own words.

When students have little experience retelling, some may give short, factual responses whereas others may provide longer, more thoughtful answers. The difference between these two students may be their comprehension of the story or it may be that one student is more verbal than the other.

Students need to be coached in how to provide a "retelling." Figure 4.1 is a graphic that teachers use to help students remember all the components of retelling. Through modeling, prompting, and opportunities to practice, students learn to provide a comprehensive "retelling." The quality of their responses is then related more to the level of their comprehension than to their inclination to be verbal.

Figure 4.1. Be a Star at Retelling

Retelling Using All Four Levels of Reading Comprehension

The six elements in Figure 4.1 connect to all four levels of reading comprehension: Initial Understanding, Developing an Interpretation, Making Connections, and Critical Stance. Steps 1 through 3 call for Initial Understanding, e.g., a literal recall of information from the story. Step 4 asks the student to Develop an Interpretation of what the main idea of the story was. Step 5 asks the student to Make a Connection between the story and his own experiences, and Step 6 asks the student to Take a Critical Stance through judging whether or not he liked the story. In all cases, the student is asked to provide information from the text to explain his ideas.

After practicing retellings with the help of the graphic in Figure 4.1, the students learn to use all four levels of reading comprehension without the support of the graphic or prompts from the teacher.

A Menu of Questions to Engage Students in Retelling

Figure 4.2 presents a menu of questions relating the four levels of thinking to the elements of a story. Teachers choose a question or two from each of the four levels and tailor them to the story being read. Using the matrix reminds teachers to address all four levels of reading comprehension. When teachers use this matrix over the course of many stories, students get experience responding to a wide variety of questions.

This menu of questions can be used informally in the context of day-to-day conversations about stories. The menu can also be used to create standard reading comprehension tools for teachers.

Reading Comprehension Profiles for Benchmark Books

The questions in Figure 4.2 can be used to develop standard questions used for retelling based on benchmark books. **Benchmark books** are books used by all of the teachers in a series of grade levels to assess the level of reading comprehension of the students. An example of a set of benchmark books for grades K–2 would be a series that begins at level A and continues through level P. After the benchmark books have been selected, a team of teachers create a standard reading comprehension form, such as the one found in Figure 4.3. Questions from the menu in Figure 4.2 have been selected for each of the three books represented in that figure. Figures 4.4 through 4.7 present the set of questions for three other books in the leveled book continuum.

Note that the questions for the book, *The Hundred Penny Box,* by Sharon Bell Mathis, are all focused on the story element "Character." A set of questions can be generated that cover the spectrum of the elements of a story or the questions can be more focused. In either case, questions at all four levels of comprehension are written.

Figure 4.2. Menu of Questions Relating the Four Levels of Thinking to the Elements of a Story

by Mike Hibbard and Beth Wagner

Add the following to the questions as necessaray: "Explain," "Find three details from the text to support your ideas." Add or exchange the word, "illustrator" to selected questions that use the word, "author."

Level of Thinking	Character Who	Setting Where, When	Events What, How	Purpose Why
Initial Understanding (i.e., describe, sequence, list)	• Who is the main character? • Who are the other characters? • What words does the author use to describe _____ (name the character)?	• Where does the story take place? • When does the story take place? • What words does the author use to describe the setting?	• What are the main events in the story? • What happened in the beginning? In the middle? At the end? • What was the problem? (The problem may be obvious or it may need to be inferred.)	• What does the title tell us about this story? • What does the book cover illustration tell us about the story?
Developing an Interpretation (i.e., infer, predict, generalize, analyze, cause and effect, compare, contrast)	• How do you know that _____ (name the character) is _____ (state character trait such as friendly, brave, honest)? • If we know that _____ (name the character) is _____ (state the character trait) what do you think that _____ (name the character) would do if _____ (describe the new situation)? • How do you think that _____ (name a character) felt about _____ (name a character or an event)? • When _____ (name a character) said _____, what do you think he/she meant? • What do you think that _____ (name a character) was thinking when _____ (name an event)? • What do you think the word _____ (or phrase) _____ means? How do you know?	• What do you think the word _____ (or phrase) _____ means? How do you know? • What is the most important thing about the setting? • Why was _____ (mention a part of the setting) a part of the setting? • How would the story have changed if _____ (mention a part of the setting) was left out of the story?	• Why did _____ (describe the event) happen? • Why did _____ (name character) _____ (state event)? • What caused _____? • How did _____ (name a character) get _____ (name a thing)? • Why do you think that it was important that _____ happened in the story? • What do you think the word _____ (or phrase) _____ means? How do you know? • At the end of the story, when _____ (describe an event or something said), what did it mean? • If _____ (name an event) had not happened, how would the story have turned out differently?	• What lesson did the author want us to learn from this story? (This is the implicit purpose.) • What do you think the word _____ (or phrase) _____ means? How do you know? • Why did the author tell us about _____ (describe what the author told) in this story? • How did the title of the story relate to the purpose of this story?

Level of Thinking	Character	Setting	Events	Purpose and Overall
Making Connections (i.e., compare, contrast)	• How was _____ (name a character) like (different from) _____ (name another character in the story)? • What was the relationship between _____ (name a character) and _____ (name another character)? • How is _____ (name the character) like _____ (name a character from another book)? • How is _____ (name the character) like you?	• How is the setting for this story like the setting of _____ (name the other story)? • How is the setting for this story like _____ (name the real setting that the child experiences)?	• How is the problem in this story like a problem in a story you have read before? • How is the problem in this story like a problem you may have had? • How is your experience the same or different from a character's in this story? • What do you think would happen between _____ (name one character) and _____ (name another character) if _____ (describe a new situation that would require the two characters to solve a similar problem.) • If you were in this situation, what would you have done? Why?	• How is the lesson of this story like the lesson from another story you have read? • How is the lesson of this story like a lesson you have learned in real life?
Critical Stance (i.e., judge, evaluate, rate)	• Did the author do a good job of showing us that _____ (name the character) was _____ (state the character trait)? • Did the author do a good job of making _____ (name the character) seem like a real little boy/girl? • Did the author do a good job making _____ (name the character) an interesting character? • Did the author do a good job making _____ (name the character) believable? • Why did the author use details about _____ (name some aspect of the character)?	• Did the author do a good job of making the setting seem real? • How did the author use _____ (state the literary device) to help you understand the setting? • Why did the author use details about _____ (name some aspect of the setting)? • Did the author do a good job making the setting believable?	• Did the author do a good job of making the story interesting? • Did the author do a good job of presenting a problem and then showing how it was solved? • Did the author do a good job of telling about a problem that we could have? • If this story continued, what do you think would happen next? • How did the author use _____ (state the literary device) to make the story interesting to you? • Why did the author use details about _____ (name some aspect of the plot)? • Was this story as good as _____ (list the title of another story)? Explain.	• Is the lesson of this story an important lesson to learn? • What do you think is important to the author? • What do you think the author is like as a person? • What customs and celebrations, are important to the author? • Was the title a good one for this story? • What would a better title be for this story? • Did the author do a good job making the story believable? • Did the author make any mistakes in telling this story? • How would you make this story better? • Overall, was this a good book? Would you recommend this book to a friend? • Would you want to read other books by this author?

Figure 4.3. Benchmark Book, *Biscuit*

Benchmark Book Title: **Biscuit**   *Guided Reading Level:* D–E
Author: *Alyssa Satin Capucilli*   *Illustrator:* Pat Schories
Text Selected By ___ Teacher ___ Student   Date: _____
Student Name: _____ Grade: ___ Teacher: _____
Number of Words: 131, Error Rate: _____ Accuracy Rate: _____ % Self Correction Rate: _____
Levels of Thinking: IU = Initial Understanding   DI = Developing an Interpretation
              MC = Making Connections   CS = Critical Stances

Questions for This Book

Level of Thinking	Character	Setting	Events	Purpose and Overall
IU	Who is Biscuit?	Where did Biscuit go to sleep?	What did Biscuit want?	
DI	How do you think that the little girl felt about Biscuit?		Do you think that the author likes animals?	
MC		What are some of the nice things that you have done for a pet?		
CS	Do you think that the author did a good job of showing what a puppy is really like?			

Amount of Prompting Required by the Teacher
_____ Much _____ Some _____ Little _____ None

Rubric Score
           Initial Understanding   _____
           Developing an Interpretation _____
           Making Connections   _____
           Critical Stance   _____
               Total   _____

Phrasing and Fluency
Read: __word by word __in short phrases   __ in longer phrases __punctuation
Reread for: __ *phrasing*   __ *punctuation*
Expresion: __emerging   __developing
Reading Rate:
__ slow ___ inconsistent __ adequate __ too fast __ adjusting appropriately

At difficulty, the student problem-solved using:
__ pictures   __ rereading   __ letter/sound __ letter/sound chunks
__ syllables   __ multiple attempts   __ pausing   __ no observable behaviors

Reading Level: __ Independent   __ Instructional __ Difficult

Figure 4.4. Benchmark Book, *Leo the Late Bloomer*

Benchmark Book Title: **Leo the Late Bloomer**   *Guided Reading Level: G*
Author: Robert Kraus   *Illustrator:* Jose Aruego

Questions for This Book

Level of Thinking	Character	Setting	Events	Purpose and Overall
IU	Who did Leo play with?	Where did this story take place?	What are the things that Leo could not do?	
DI	Was Leo a happy tiger?		At the end of the story Leo said, "I made it." What did he mean?	
MC			Are you an early bloomer, a regular bloomer, or a late bloomer?	
CS				Do you think that the author thinks it is OK to be a late bloomer?

Figure 4.5. Benchmark Book, Peeping and Sleeping

Benchmark Book Title: **Peeping and Sleeping**
Guided Reading Level: I
Author: Fran Manushkin   *Illustrator: Jennifer Piecas*

Questions for This Book

Level of Thinking	Character	Setting	Events	Purpose and Overall
IU	Who was the main character?	Describe where this story took place.	Tell me what happened when Barry went back to his house and went to bed.	
DI	How do you know that Barry was a brave boy?			What was the author telling us about how fathers help sons?
MC		How could you use a flashlight like Barry did?		
CS				Why was the title "Peeping and Sleeping" a good title for this story?

Figure 4.6. Benchmark Book, *The Mitten*

Benchmark Book Title: **The Mitten**   *Guided Reading Level:* M
Author: Alvin Tresselt   *Illustrator:* Yaroslava

Questions for This Book

Level of Thinking	Character	Setting	Events	Purpose and Overall
IU		Where did the story take place? Tell me all about that place.	Why did the mitten tear?	
DI	Were the animals selfish or unselfish? Find three details in the story that prove your point.			What purpose did the author have for telling this folktale?
MC			Have you ever had the experience of losing something and wondering what happened to it? Tell me about it.	
CS			Did the author do a good job of using fantasy in this story? Explain.	

Figure 4.7. Benchmark Book, The Hundred Penny Box

Benchmark Book Title: **The Hundred Penny Box**   *Guided Reading Level:* P
Author: Sharon Bell Mathis   *Illustrator:* Leo and Diane Dillon

Questions for This Book

Level of Thinking	Character	Setting	Events	Purpose and Overall
IU	What did Aunt Dew look like? Find at least three pieces of information from the story to support your description.			
DI	Why was the hundred penny box important to Aunt Dew?			
MC	What experiences have you had with elderly people? How were they like or different from Aunt Dew?			
CS	Do you think the author did a good job of making Aunt Dew seem real? Find at least three pieces of information from the story to support your opinion.		If the author made the story longer, what would Michael and Aunt Dew do next?	

Analytic Rubric for Assessing Retelling

Each reading comprehension profile has the following section to record data from the assessment of the student's responses to retelling questions in each of the four areas of reading comprehension:

Rubric Score

Initial Understanding   _____

Developing an Interpretation   _____

Making Connections   _____

Critical Stance   _____

Total   _____

A rubric is needed to provide a rating for each of these four levels of comprehension.

Figure 4.8 presents the rubric used to assess student performance. After the student has finished retelling, the teacher will give the student a score on each of the four levels of comprehension. The student gets one overall score for Initial Understanding, one overall score for Developing an Interpretation, one overall score for Making Connections, and one overall score for Critical Stance. The four scores are summed to give an overall reading comprehension score. If the student scores at the top end of "Adequate Comprehension" Level (see the box in the upper right-hand corner of the rubric in Figure 4.8) then this book is probably at the right level for that student.

Figure 4.8   Retelling Comprehension Rubric   by Mike Hibbard, Beth Wagner and Jason McKinnon

Name _____ Date: _____

Text _____

Scoring: Each Comprehension Strand (IU, DI, MC, and CS) has four levels of quality. Mark one level of performance for each of the four strands. You will have marked four of the boxes – one for each strand. The points for each level of quality are indicated at the top of the rubric. Calculate the number of total points the student has earned. The box titled Comprehension Level shows how to convert a score to a description of the comprehension level.

Comprehension Level	
Scoring: Record student's total score in the appropriate category	
Very Good Comprehension	❑ 15-16
Adequate Comprehension	❑ 11-14
Some Comprehension	❑ 7-10
Very Little Comprehension	❑ 4-6

	1 point	2 points	3 points	4 points
Comprehension Strand	**Very Little Comprehension**	**Some Comprehension**	**Adequate Comprehension**	**Very Good Comprehension**
IU *Initial Understanding*	* Includes few details. Leaves out most of the plot (beginning, middle, end) * Refers to characters with pronouns: (he, she, it) * Uses little or no descriptive language. * Some information accurate and some inaccurate	* Includes important details that are mostly in sequence. May leave out some parts of plot. * Uses generic names for characters and places, i.e., the boy, the dog, the store *Provides some details * Most information accurate	* Includes the most important details in sequences * Uses specific names of characters and places * Provides most of the details in the text * Uses descriptive language and all information accurate	* Shows a clear sense of plot through excellent details presented in order. * Uses specific names of characters and places *Provides all details and elaborates info. accurately * Uses descriptive language exceptionally well and accurately.
DI *Developing Interpretation*	* Very little ability to make inferences * Predictions not related to the story * Little or no understanding of the most obvious cause and effect relationships. * Little ability to explain the author's use of words or phrases in the story	* Inferences are weak. Supported with some info. * Predictions are not supported well from the text *Shows some understanding of the most obvious cause and effect relationships. * Some ability to explain the author's use of words or phrases in the story	* Makes and supports inferences with specific info. from the text * Makes predictions and supports with evidence * Shows clear understanding of cause and effect relationships in story * Clear ability to explain the author's use of words or phrases in the story	*Shows exceptional insight regarding inferences * Provides exceptional support for predictions * Shows exceptional insight into cause and effect relationships * Provides deeper than normal interpretations of words and phrases to present the characters and/ or "teach a lesson."
MC *Making Connections*	* Has difficulty making comparisons and/or contrasts * Few supporting details are used to explain the similarities and/or differences in the text.	* Uses some details to support comparisons and contrasts. * Uses little descriptive language when making comparisons and contrasts.	*Uses numerous details to make comparisons and contrasts: Text-to-Text, Text-to-Self, Text-to-World. *Uses specific words and phrases from the text * Uses descriptive language to explain similarities and differences	* Uses many, accurate details and key vocabulary from text to make comparisons and contrasts * Creates metaphors and/or similes to explain similarities and/or differences
CS *Critical Stance*	* Presents a very general opinion of the story such as, "I like it…" but provides little or no details to explain	*Presents, with difficulty, a personal opinion to evaluate or judge the author's and/or illustrator's work *Has difficulty using specific details from the text to support the evaluation or judgment	* Presents a personal opinion to evaluate or judge the quality of the author's work *Uses specific details to support the evaluation *Shows a good understanding of the author's purpose and style. Is able to extend the story or apply meaning	*Uses exceptionally specific details to support an evaluation or judgment. *Demonstrates a deeper understanding of the author's use of words, phrases, and purpose * An understanding of the author's values and opinions.

References

Level D-E: *Biscuit* by Alyssa Satin Capucilli pictures by Pat Schories, 1996. New York: Harper Collins Children'd Books.

Level G: Kraus, R. (1971). *Leo the Late Bloomer* (pictures by Jose Aruego). New York: Harper Collins Children's Books.

Level I: Manushkin, F. (1994). *Peeping and Sleeping* (J. Plecas, Illus.). New York: Houghton Mifflin.

Level M: Tresselt, A. (1964). *The Mitten* (Yaroslava, Illus.). New York: Lothrop, Lee & Shepard.

Level P: Bell Mathis, S. (1975). *The Hundred Penny Box* (L. Dillon & D. Dillon, Illus.). New York: Penguin Books.

5

Connecting Standards and Themes to Performance Tasks

Topics for This Chapter

♦ The Standards for English Language Arts will be presented. The connections between each standard and the strategies to teach and assess reading comprehension in this book and in volume one in the two-set series, *Assessing and Teaching Reading Comprehension and Pre-Writing, K–3*, will be explained.

♦ Samples of themes and essential questions for fiction and nonfiction texts will be provided.

♦ Three sets of performance tasks will be presented with explanations as to how they connect to standards and themes/essential questions.

Standards for English Language Arts

Standards are guidelines for what students should know and be able to do. English Language Arts standards address process skills that are related to the writing process and address content, such as how and why beliefs and values are expressed in literature. Although standards are presented as "lists," giving the impression of discrete items, the standards should always be thought of as highly interrelated. Any one learning activity or assessment is a mix of several standards.

The standards presented here are from the National Council of Teachers of English as published in Crafton, L. K. (1996). *Standards in Practice: Grades K–2.* Urbana, IL: National Council of Teachers of English.

As stated by Linda Crafton, "Although we present these standards as a list, we want to emphasize that they are not distinct and separable; they are, in fact, interrelated and should be considered as a whole."

The italicized text explains the connections between the English Language Arts (ELA) Standards and the strategies and materials for assessing reading comprehension and writing in this book.

ELA1. Read a Wide Range of Texts for Many Purposes: Students read a wide range of print and nonprint text to build an understanding of texts, of themselves, and of the cultures of the United States and the world; to acquire new information; to respond to the needs and demands of society and the workplace; and for personal fulfillment. Among these texts are fiction and nonfiction, classic, and contemporary works.

This book includes a wide range of fiction and nonfiction books, including leveled books, as the basis for the development of performance tasks.

ELA2. Read Texts from Many Genres to Understand People: Students read a wide range of literature from many periods and in many genres to build an understanding of the many dimensions (e.g., philosophical, ethical, aesthetic) of human experience.

This book includes a range of genres. The strategies and materials presented here are applicable to an even wider range.

ELA3. Use a Variety of Flexible Comprehension Strategies: Students apply a wide range of strategies to comprehend, interpret, evaluate, and appreciate texts. They draw on their prior experience, their interactions with other readers and writers, their knowledge of word meaning and other texts, their word identification strategies, and their understanding of textual features (e.g., sound-letter correspondence, sentence structure, contexts, and graphics.)

The thinking-skill verbs from the four levels of reading comprehension, Initial Understanding, Developing an Interpretation, Making Connections, and Critical Stance, define a comprehensive approach to comprehension. The use of drawings and graphic organizers as final products of performance tasks or pre-writing activities prepares the student for a final written product and provides a set of flexible comprehension strategies. The application of self-assessment as an integral part of all performance tasks helps the students to become self-reflective, independent learners.

ELA4. Write, Speak, and Draw to Communicate with Specific Audiences: Students adjust their use of spoken, written, and visual language (e.g., conventions, style, or vocabulary) to communicate effectively with a variety of audiences and for different purposes.

Each performance task has an audience for the student's work. Sometimes the audience, such as the principal, parent, or firefighter is real or authentic, and sometimes the audience, like Little Bear, is pretend.

ELA5. Use a Wide Range of Writing Strategies to Communicate with Different Audiences for Different Purposes: Students employ a wide range of strategies as they write and use different writing process elements appropriately to communicate with different audiences for a variety of purposes.

Drawings, graphic organizers, sentences, narrative and expository paragraphs, multiparagraph stories, and multiparagraph expository pieces provide some range of strategies. Journal writing, self-reflections and goal setting in portfolios add to that range.

ELA6. Use Knowledge of the Structure and Mechanics of Language: Students apply knowledge of language structure, language conventions (e.g., spelling and punctuation), media techniques, figurative language, and genre to create, critique, and discuss print and nonprint texts.

All analytic rubrics for writing include the structure and mechanics of language. Assessment list items apply the information in analytic rubrics to performance tasks.

ELA7. Find Information through Research: Students conduct research on issues and interests by generating ideas and questions, and by posing problems. They gather, evaluate, and synthesize data from a variety of sources (e.g., print and nonprint texts, artifacts, people) to communicate their discoveries in ways that suit their purposes and audience.

All performance tasks that ask students to go back to the text(s) to find evidence and information for their work on performance tasks encourage "research." Several performance tasks in this book engage students in asking questions, finding and evaluating information sources, organizing that information, and writing final reports.

ELA8. Use a Variety of Information Resources for Research: Students use a variety of technological and informational resources (e.g., libraries, databases, computer networks, videos) to gather and synthesize information and to create and communicate knowledge.

This book focuses on the use of fiction and nonfiction texts, but the strategies and materials can easily incorporate all other types of information sources.

ELA9. Learn about Diversity: Students develop an understanding of, and respect for, diversity in language use, patterns, and dialects across cultures, ethnic groups, geographic regions, and social roles.

The strategies and materials for creating performance tasks and assessment lists in this book can easily be used to encourage learning and assess comprehension of issues around diversity.

ELA10. English as a Second Language: Students whose first language is not English make use of their first language to develop competency in the English language arts and to develop understanding of content across the curriculum.

This book focuses entirely on English. Graphic organizers are available in other languages such as Spanish. Spanish speaking students can begin a performance task by using the Spanish version of a graphic organizer and then translate the Spanish into English in another graphic organizer. Thus, pre-writing is begun in Spanish and completed in English.

ELA11. **Participate as a Reader and Writer with Various People**: Students participate as knowledgeable, reflective, creative, and critical members of a variety of literacy communities.

Many performance tasks in this book ask students to read their final work to audiences such as the principal, librarian, parent, art teacher, younger students, their reading group partners, or an author's group.

ELA12. **Accomplish One's Own Purposes with Language**: Students use spoken, written , and visual language to accomplish their own purposes (e.g., for learning, enjoyment, persuasion, and the exchange of information.)

Every performance task asks students to craft their work to have an "impact" on their audience. The students plan how to teach, inform, or entertain their audience.

Themes, Essential Questions, and Focus Questions

Themes, Essential Questions, and Focus Questions are used to define the content of a performance task.

Theme: Themes are the "big ideas" that are important to a discipline. A theme important to literature is "How are the elements of a story structured?" A science theme is, "What are the patterns in nature?" and a social studies theme is, "How do the relationships people have with each other change them?"

Essential Question: An essential question directs learning to an important aspect of a theme. Figure 5.1 shows essential questions for the three examples of themes.

Focus Question: A focus question for a performance task is directly connected to an essential question. Figure 5.1 shows the relationship among the theme, essential question, and focus question.

Note that themes, essential questions, and focus questions are all written in the form of questions. Questions call for answers, and the purpose of themes, essential questions, and focus questions is to direct active thinking.

Figure 5.1. The Flow from Theme to Essential Question to Focus Question

Theme *The most abstract level.*	Essential Question *More specific than the theme.*	Focus Question *The question for a performance task.*
How are the elements of a story structured to tell a story? (Literature)	How is the story structured to have a beginning, middle and ending?	What are the important events in the beginning, middle, and ending of the story *Cherries and Cherry Pits*?
What are the patterns in nature? (Science)	How does a food web work?	What part do spiders play in the food web?
How do the relationships people have with each other affect them? (Social Studies)	How do friends treat one another?	How would Little Bear treat you if he was your friend?

The emphasis in previous chapters has been on thinking-skills verbs, processing information with the help of graphic organizers, and the process of writing. The content and information from the student's reading must also be incorporated into performance tasks and assessed. The most common problems with performance tasks are that they are too long, take too much class time, focus on process skills, such as thinking skills and the writing process, and do not pay enough attention to the content of what has been learned.

Each performance task must focus both on the content of what has been learned and on the process skills used to complete the work of the performance task. Each performance task must ask the students to demonstrate the depth of their understanding of content, to exhibit their skill in processing information according to a thinking-skill verb, and to show their skill in using the writing process to communicate their ideas to others.

The following are some suggestions for how to use themes, essential questions, and focus questions to define the content of the performance task.

Fiction

The content of fiction is usually related to the theme of the story, the elements and structure of a story, the traits of the main characters, and the literacy devices and language used to accomplish the purposes of the story. Some themes and essential questions for literature follow.

(Note: *Themes are presented in bold typeface, and essential questions follow in italic. Some essential questions for a theme can be used with kindergarteners and first graders, and other essential questions are introduced to older children.*)
Literature = L

L1. What are the elements of a story?
   L1.1. Who are the main characters and other characters of this story?
   L1.2. What is the setting in time and place for this story?
   L1.3. What is the plot?
   L1.4. How is a story built around a theme?

L2. How are the elements of a story structured to tell the story?
   L2.1. What events make up the beginning, middle, and ending of the story.
   L2.3. How are plots structured around problems and their solutions?
   L2.4. How are settings in time and place created and used to tell a story?
   L2.5. How are characters created and used to tell a story?

L3. What are the attributes of human nature? (character traits)
   L3.1. From the actions a character takes, what can we infer about that character's traits? What kind of a "person" do you think this character was? Character traits include: adventuresome, arrogant, brave, charitable, competitive, cooperative, creative, dishonest, disorganized, empathetic, enthusiastic, faithful, foolish, friendly, happy, hardworking, honest, greedy, intelligent, irresponsible, kind, lazy, loyal, organized, patient, polite, prejudiced, responsible, skillful, strong, weak, and wise. What is the evidence for your opinion of what the character trait is for that character?
   L3.2. Based on your knowledge of the most important character trait(s) of the character, what do you predict the character will do when...?
   L3.3. What feelings did the character have? What is your evidence?
   L3.4. What made the character feel the way it did? What is your evidence?

L4. How are literary devices used by the author to accomplish his or her work? (Note that the essential questions here are stated in terms of taking a Critical Stance about how well the author did his or her work.)
   L4.1. Did the author do a good job creating a title that catches our interest?
   L4.2. How well did the author use descriptive language to create a picture of the setting?
   L4.3. How well did the author use action verbs to make the story interesting?
   L4.4. How well did the author use new vocabulary to make the story interesting?
   L4.5 How well did the author use dialogue to make the character(s) believable?
   L4.6 How well did the author use (fantasy, humor, metaphors, similes) to tell the story?
   L4.7. How interesting are the illustrations or photographs?

L4.8. How helpful are the illustrations/photographs in telling the story?

L4.9. How does the author's opinion, point of view, and beliefs influence their work?

L5. What are important themes of literature?

L5.1. How do people change?

L5.2. What does it mean to be human?

L5.3. Who are our heroes?

L5.4. What is truth and beauty?

L5.5. What is the struggle between good and evil?

L6. What have I learned about myself?

L6.1. What are my values?

L6.2. What is important to me?

L6.3. What do I want to be?

Nonfiction

The content of nonfiction is more than factual information. It includes big ideas and essential questions that help specific facts fit together and be remembered. For example, one big idea is, "What are the patterns in nature?" An essential question for this theme is, "How do food chains work?" When students study spiders, a focus question relevant to this essential question could be, "What part do spiders play in the food chain?"

As students study other living things, focus questions will ask about how each type of living thing fits into a food chain. After several experiences with specific food webs, the concept of food chains becomes more meaningful, and students will use it in their independent view of the world. When focus questions about food chains are used, the teacher also reminds the student of the essential question and the theme from which it was derived. Students always see the relationship between themes, essential questions, and focus questions.

When using themes, essential questions, and focus questions, the study of nonfiction topics rises above the accumulation of facts to the deeper understanding of ideas that are useful throughout life. The themes are general and apply across a very wide range of topics. The essential questions are specific to a particular topic and written so that the students who use them can understand them. The focus question is what students think about during a performance task.

The following are examples of themes and essential questions relevant to the some of the nonfiction texts referenced in this book.

(Note: *Themes are presented in bold typeface, and essential questions follow in italic.*)

S=Science SS=Social Studies

S1. How do the external and internal structures of living things help them accomplish their life functions in specific environments?

S1.1. How is the skeleton structured so that an animal can move?

S1.2. How is the skeleton structured to protect an animal's soft parts?

S1.3. How does the structures of an animal help it catch and eat food?

S1.4. How do the structures of plants help them get what they need to live?

S1.5. How do the structures of animals help protect the animals?

S1.6. How do the body parts of an animal help it know about its environment?

S1.7. How do the structures of plants help protect the plant?

S1.8. How do the structures of an animal help it adapt to its environment?

S1.9. How do the structures of a plant help it adapt to its environment?

S1.10. How do the structures that animals make help them survive in their environment?

S2. How are physical systems organized and how do they work?

S2.1. What is the structure of an atom and a molecule?

S2.2. How are atoms and molecules the "building blocks" of life?

S2.3. What is the structure of the earth?

S2.4. What happens to the earth because of its structure?

S2.5. What is the structure of our solar system?

S2.6. What happens in our solar system because of its structure?

S3. What patterns can be found in nature?

S3.1. What is the water cycle and how does it work?

S3.2. What is a food chain and how does it work?

S3.3. What is the life cycle of a plant?

S3.4. What is the life cycle of an animal?

S3.5. What cycles are there in the weather and what causes them?

S3.6. What is the rock cycle and how does it work?

S3.7. How do the water cycle and the rock cycle fit together?

SS1. How do geography, climate, and the weather affect the way people live?

SS1.1. How do patterns in the weather influence how people live? How do patterns in the weather influence the way plants and animals live?

SS1.2. How does water influence how people live? How does water influence the way that plants and animals live?

SS1.3. How does temperature influence how people live? How does the temperature influence how plants and animals live?

SS1.4. How does the geography of an area influence how people live? How does the geography influence how plants and animals live in that area?

SS1.5. How important are rivers to people?

SS2. How does the division of labor in a community help every one?

SS2.1. What are the different jobs that people do and how are those jobs important?

SS2.2. Why is it important that different people do different jobs?

SS2.3. How does working together help all of us?

SS3. **How do the relationships people have with each other affect them?**
SS3.1. How do people in families show they care for one another?
SS3.2. How do people behave towards one another when they are friends?
SS3.3. How do people who are on teams help each other?
SS3.4. How do people who work together help each other?

SS4. **How and why do people use stories, art, songs, dances, food, holidays, and celebrations to tell what they believe and value?**
SS3.1. Why do people have holidays?
SS3.2. How do people use stories, art, songs, dances, and food to show what is important about that holiday?
SS3.3. How do stories, fables, myths, and legends show what people believe?
SS3.4. How do people show what they believe and feel in their art?
SS3.5. How do people show what they believe and feel in their music?

Why Are Themes, Essential Questions, and Focus Questions Written as Questions?

There are two reasons why themes and essential questions are stated as questions rather than statements. First, questions stimulate thinking and the search for answers. Second, because we want students to learn to ask questions to direct their thinking, we should learn to use questions to structure teaching and learning as a model to show this way of thinking. Note that all of the ideas for performance tasks in this book have been presented in the form of questions.

Questions call for answers. The question, "**How does the division of labor in a community help everyone?**" is more thought provoking than the statement, "**Division of Labor.**" Likewise, the question, "**What patterns can be found in nature?**" asks us to search for answers, whereas the word, "**Patterns**" gives us a label but does not move us as strongly towards inquiry.

Ideas for Performance Tasks and Their Connections to Standards and Themes/Essential Questions

Figure 5.2 presents ideas for performance tasks based on the Little Bear books and on a collection of nonfiction books about spiders. Each idea for a performance task includes the thinking-skill verb, the relevant English Language Arts standards, and the relevant theme(s) and essential question(s).

The English Language Arts standards connect the performance task to the processes of reading and communicating. All ideas for performance tasks connect to many of the English Language Arts standards. Each of the performance tasks that are created from these ideas will ask students to read texts for specific purposes; use a variety of comprehension strategies; communicate through speaking, drawing, and writing; communicate with specific audiences for specific purposes, use knowledge of the structure and mechanics of language; and find information through research.

One of the common shortcomings of performance tasks is that they emphasize process skills and have very little "content." Connecting the performance task to at least one theme and essential question in at least one discipline helps to ensure rich content in the performance task. This connection defines the "content" of the performance task. For example, one task about Little Bear is connected to the literature theme, "What are the attributes of human nature?" and its essential question is, "What is the most important character trait of Little Bear?" A performance task idea for *Cherries and Cherry Pits* is connected to the science theme, "What patterns can be found in nature?" and its essential question is, "What is the life cycle of a plant?" Some performance tasks are connected to themes and essential questions in more than one discipline.

Figure 5.2. Ideas For Performance Tasks And Connections To Standards, Themes, And Essential Questions

ELA = English Language Arts   T = Theme   EQ = Essential Question

Book	Focus Questions (Ideas) For Performance Tasks (thinking skill verb in parenthesis)	English Language Arts Standard	Literature		Science		Social Studies	
			T	EQ	T	EQ	T	EQ
A Kiss for Little Bear	Who got a kiss in the book, A Kiss for Little Bear? (Initial Understanding: List)	ELA1, 2, 3,11,12	L1	L1.1				
Little Bear's Friend	How would you and Little Bear be friends if you met on the school playground? (Developing An Interpretation: Predict)	ELA1, 2, 3, 4, 11, 12	L3	L3.2			SS3	SS3.2
Various Little Bear books.	Is Little Bear a friendly, kind member of the Bear family? Pick one and find evidence from at least two Little Bear books and explain. (Making Connections: Infer)	ELA1, 2, 3, 4, 7, 11, 12	L3	L3.1			SS3	SS3.1 SS3.2
	Do you think that the author, Else Holmelund Minarik, likes animals? How do you know? Find evidence from at least two books and explain. (Critical Stance: Judge)	ELA1, 2, 3, 4, 7, 11, 12	L4	L4.10				
Cherries and Cherry Pits	What is Bidemmi's talent? Draw a picture showing Bidemmi's talent. Describe what she is doing. (Initial Understanding: Describe)	ELA1, 2, 3, 4, 5, 7, 11, 12	L3	L3.1			SS4	SS4.4
	How could you be like Bidemmi and show your love for some kind of food? Tell a story like Cherries and Cherry Pits but use a different fruit. You are the main character in your story. (Developing an Interpretation: Extend)	ELA1, 2, 3, 4, 5, 7, 11, 12	L1 L2	L1.1 L1.2 L1.3 L2.1 L2.2				

Book	Focus Questions (Ideas) For Performance Tasks (thinking skill verb in parenthesis)	English Language Arts Standard	Literature T	Literature EQ	Science T	Science EQ	Social Studies T	Social Studies EQ
Cherries and Cherry Pits	What is the same about the life cycles of a cherry tree in the book and a bean plant that we grew in our classroom? (Making Connection: Comparing)	ELA1, 2, 3, 4, 5, 7, 8, 11, 12			S3	S3.3		
	Did the author Vera B. Williams do a good job of teaching us about Bidemmi through the watercolor paintings she did in the book Cherries and Cherry Pits? (Critical Stance: Judge)	ELA1, 2, 3, 4, 5, 7, 11, 12	L4	L4.8				
Various Books On Spiders	What different kinds of webs do spiders spin? Draw at least thee kinds of webs and draw the type of spider that spins them. (Initial Understanding: Describe)	ELA1, 2, 3, 4, 5, 7, 8, 11, 12			S1	S1.10		
	What are the parts of a spider and what do those parts do to help the spider catch and eat food? (Developing An Interpretation: Explain)	ELA1, 2, 3, 4, 5, 7, 8, 11, 12			S1	S1.3		
	What are the differences and similarities between spiders and insects? Pick one of these topics and explain the similarities and differences between spiders and insects. How do they move? How do they eat? How do they know what is going on around them? (Making Connections: Compare and Contrast)	ELA1, 2, 3, 4, 5, 7, 8, 11, 12			S1	S1.1 S1.2 S1.3 S1.5 S1.8		
	Which book about spiders was the best book for your research? Why? (Critical Stance: Evaluate)	ELA1, 2, 3, 4, 5, 7, 8, 11, 12			S1 S3	Depends on the student's research question.		

The Sequence of Activities in a Performance Task Follows the Writing Process

Figure 5.3 takes those same ideas for tasks and continues the planning to show what kinds of pre-writing activities—such as drawings and graphic organizers—will be used and what kind of final written product will be called for. Performance tasks for students who are less experienced with the writing process will have a drawing or a graphic organizer as the final product. The performance tasks begin with drawings and/or graphic organizers and then move to a final written product as the students gain experience and expertise with the writing process.

These performance tasks are structured to support the writing process. Each step of the writing process has its own product and assessment list. The tasks that include only a drawing or graphic organizer have only one assessment list. The performance tasks that have drawings and/or graphic organizers and final written products have a series of assessment lists—one for each product during the performance task. Each of these assessment lists is used as a "stop and check" point for the students and teachers to assure that they are on track with their work.

Sometimes the teacher will do the planning stages of a performance task in small groups and then let each individual do his or her own final product. This strategy is especially useful when students are making the transition from one-step tasks to multi-step tasks. For example, the performance task entitled, "Life Cycle," presented in Figures 5.9a through 5.9e could begin in cooperative groups and could be finished by individuals. The graphic organizers for the life cycle of a cherry, the graphic organizer for the life cycle of a bean, and the graphic organizer used to plan the explanation, could be done in cooperative groups. The final written explanation would then be done by each individual student. When students have experience with mult-istep tasks, then all of the pre-writing steps would be done by each individual.

Planning Thinking-Skill Verbs for Performance Tasks

Thinking-skill verbs from the four levels of reading comprehension—Initial Understanding, Developing an Interpretation, Making Connections, and Critical Stance—are used in every performance task. For the primary grades, only one thinking-skill verb should be used for a single performance task. For example, a performance task may use the verb "sequence" to focus on putting the events in the story in the correct order. Or the task may use the verb "infer" to focus on finding evidence about the character traits of a main character. It is not recommended that one performance task be created that includes both verbs, "sequence" and "infer," because that would make the performance task too complicated and long for students in the primary grades.

Figure 5.3. Planning the Components of Performance Tasks

IU = Initial Understanding   MC = Making Connections   N = Narrative
DI = Developing An Interpretation   CS = Critical Stance   E = Expository

Book Title	Task Title (Same tasks as listed in Figure 5.2.)	Thinking Skill Verb	Pre-writing Product Drawing	Pre-writing Product Graphic Organizer	Sentence	Paragraph N	Paragraph E	Multi-Paragraph N	Multi-Paragraph E
A Kiss For Little Bear	Who Got A Kiss?	IU List			X				
	You And Little Bear	DU Predict		GO34		X			
Various Little Bear Books	Little Bear And The Bear Family	MC Infer		GO11			X		
	Does The Author Like Animals?	CS Judge		GO27			X		
Cherries and Cherry Pits	What Was Bidemmi's Talent?	IU Describe	X				X		
	Following The Example Of Bidemmi	DU Extend		GO31 GO32 GO36				X	
	Life Cycle	MC Compare		GO8 GO41					X
	A Picture Is Worth A Thousand Words	CS Judge		GO24			X		
Various Books On Spiders	Amazing Webs	IU Describe	X	GO41			X		
	Spider Body Parts	DU Explain	X	GO41					X
	Comparing Insects And Spiders	MC Compare Contrast	X	GO19 GO41					X
	Resources For Research	CS Evaluate		GO40 GO39 GO31					X

Using a Series of Performance Tasks

The performance tasks presented in this chapter on the topic of spiders are created to be a four-part set of tasks. This set shows how several performance tasks can be used in the context of a whole unit of instruction that includes many activities—several of which are performance tasks. The student draws and explains how spider webs work, draws and explains how the structure of a spider helps it live and get food, draws and explains the similarities and differences between insects and spiders, and, finally, plans and conducts a simple research project about spiders. All of the work from these tasks for each student is saved and bound together into a student's "Spider Book." When the Spider Book is completed, the student meets with their kindergarten buddy and teaches them about spiders.

Using a Performance Task Planning Form

Figure 5.4 presents a form used by teachers to plan performance tasks, and Figure 5.5 shows the planning for the performance task entitled, "Spider Body Parts." Including the theme, essential question, and focus question assures a strong connection to content. The thinking-skill verb "explain" was chosen from the category "Developing an Interpretation" (DI). A drawing and graphic organizer GO41 will involve pre-writing activities leading to a multiparagraph expository paper. The audience for this work is the student's "Kindergarten Buddy" and the purpose of the work is to teach the kindergartener about spiders. Overall, the teacher has selected Self-Assessment as the work habit on which to focus.

Figure 5.4. Planning Performance Tasks

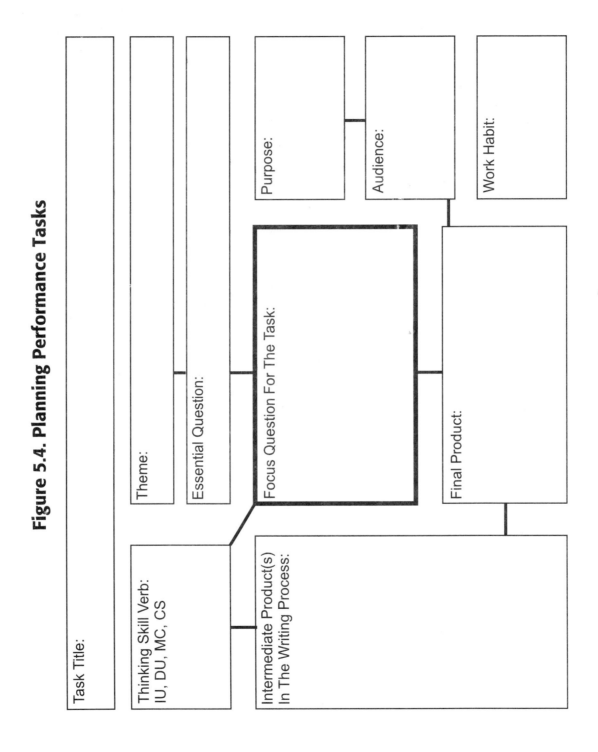

Task Title:

Theme:

Essential Question:

Thinking Skill Verb:
IU, DU, MC, CS

Focus Question For The Task:

Purpose:

Audience:

Work Habit:

Final Product:

Intermediate Product(s)
In The Writing Process:

Figure 5.5. Planning Performance Tasks

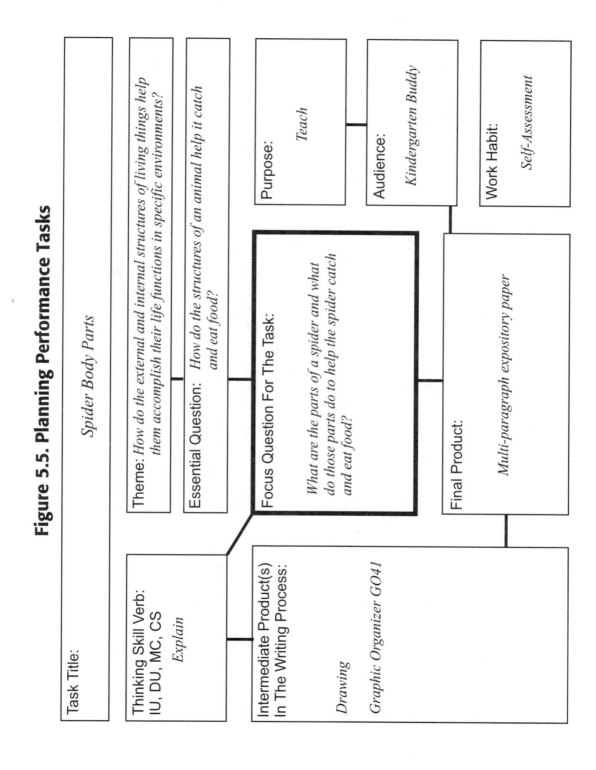

Task Title: *Spider Body Parts*

Theme: *How do the external and internal structures of living things help them accomplish their life functions in specific environments?*

Essential Question: *How do the structures of an animal help it catch and eat food?*

Focus Question For The Task: *What are the parts of a spider and what do those parts do to help the spider catch and eat food?*

Thinking Skill Verb: IU, DU, MC, CS *Explain*

Intermediate Product(s) In The Writing Process: *Drawing* *Graphic Organizer GO41*

Final Product: *Multi-paragraph expository paper*

Purpose: *Teach*

Audience: *Kindergarten Buddy*

Work Habit: *Self-Assessment*

Creating Assessment Lists
for Performance Tasks

Guidelines for creating assessment lists include:

- Put only as many items on the assessment list as students will pay attention to.

- Create a short assessment list for each component of the performance task. Assessment lists for the drawing, the graphic organizer, and the final written paragraph can all be used with a performance task. The assessment lists provide the opportunity for a "stop and check" by the student and the teacher at each step along the way.

- State the items as questions the student would ask himself.

- Make some items specific such as, "Did I use five colors to emphasize Bidemmi's talent (in *Cherries and Cherry Pits*?" and "Did I give at least two reasons for my opinion?" Assessment list items are made this specific when the teacher wants to assure that the students know the expectations for the task.

- Include some "Sure Thing" items that reinforce what students already do very well. If students are good at writing main ideas, then a sure thing item would be, "Did I write a clear main idea?"

- Include some "Challenge" items that focus attention on newly learned skills and ideas. If the new learning has been about how to write a conclusion, then the challenge item would be, "Did I write an interesting conclusion?"

- Refer to the analytic rubrics for the kind of work students are asked to do in the performance task. Write assessment list items to reflect the parts of the analytic rubric that you want to stress. If, from your review of the analytic rubrics for narrative writing, you have determined that students need to pay attention to the structure of a story, then the assessment list item might be, "Did I have a beginning, middle, and ending to my story?" If, from your review of the analytic rubrics for expository writing, you have determined that the students need to work on the use of content-specific vocabulary, then the assessment list item might read, "Did I use at least four of the words from the vocabulary list about spiders?"

- Write some assessment list items that relate to work habits, such as writing your name on the paper, doing neat work, or getting the work done on time.

- Write assessment list items to respond to the focus question for a task. If the focus question asks, "Is Little Bear a kind member of the Bear family?" then the assessment list would include items such as, "Did I find three things that Little Bear did that shows he was a kind member of the Bear family?" If the focus question asks, "What are the parts of a spider that help the spider live?" then the assessment list would include items such as, "Did I draw the body parts of the spider that help the spider catch food?"

♦ Engage the students in helping to create assessment lists when they have enough experience.

Graphic Organizers Used for the Performance Tasks in This Chapter

Graphic organizers GO1 through GO29 are found in volume one of this two-set series, *Assessing and Teaching Reading Comprehension and Pre-Writing, K–3*. Graphic Organizers GO30 through GO43 are in Chapter 3 of this book.

Figure 5.6a. Performance Task:
You and Little Bear

see the assessment lists on pages 153 and 154

Background
The book, *Little Bear's Friend*, showed us that Little Bear was a good friend. What would it be like if you and Little Bear were friends. Imagine that Little Bear came to our school and was your friend.

Task
Write a story that shows how you and Little Bear would be friends.

Audience
You will read your story to your cooperative group.

Purpose
Your friends will enjoy hearing your story.

Procedure
1. Review the assessment lists.
2. Complete the graphic organizer GO34.
3. Write the story.
4. Check your work with the assessment lists.

Figure 5.7a. Performance Task:
Does Else Holmelund Minarik Like Animals?

see the assessment lists on pages 155 and 156

Background
Do you think that the author Else Holmelund Minarik likes animals? How can you tell?

Task
Find some evidence in her books that tells you if she likes animals or not.

Audience
You will send your paragraph to the author.

Purpose
The author will be interested in learning about what you think she likes.

Procedure
1. Review the assessment lists.
2. Compete the graphic organizer GO27.
3. Check your work with the assessment lists.

Figure 5.6b. Performance Task Assessment List: You and Little Bear (Graphic Organizer)

1. Did I give the story an interesting title?

| Terrific | OK | Needs Work |

2. Did I plan the problem that Little Bear and I would solve?

| Terrific | OK | Needs Work |

3. Did I plan what Little Bear and I did to solve our problem?

| Terrific | OK | Needs Work |

4. Did I plan the conclusion?

| Terrific | OK | Needs Work |

Figure 5.6c. Performance Task Assessment List: You and Little Bear (Story)

1. Does my story have an interesting middle that described a problem that Little Bear and I would solve together?

Terrific   OK   Needs Work

2. Does my story show and tell the action that took place?

Terrific   OK   Needs Work

3. Did my story have an interesting conclusion that showed how Little Bear and I solved the problem?

Terrific   OK   Needs Work

4. Did I use capitals correctly?

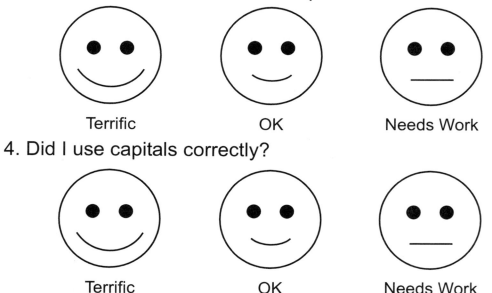

Terrific   OK   Needs Work

Figure 5.7b. Performance Task Assessment List: Does Else Holmelund Minarik Like Animals? (Graphic Organizer)

1. Did I write the question I am asking about how the author feels about animals?

Terrific   OK   Needs Work

2. Did I find at least two reasons for my opinion?

Terrific   OK   Needs Work

3. Did I write a conclusion?

Terrific   OK   Needs Work

4. Did I check my spelling?

Terrific   OK   Needs Work

Figure 5.7c. Performance Task Assessment List: Does Else Holmelund Minarik Like Animals? (Paragraph)

1. Does my main idea state my opinion clearly?

Terrific   OK   Needs Work

2. Did I give two reasons for my opinion?

Terrific   OK   Needs Work

3. Are my reasons based on evidence from the books?

Terrific   OK   Needs Work

4. Did I end my paragraph with my opinion about Little Bear?

Terrific   OK   Needs Work

Figure 5.8a. Performance Task: Following the Example of Bidemmi

see the assessment lists on pages 158, 159, 160, and 161

Background
Bidemmi planted cherry pits all over the neighborhood. The pits grew into cherry trees and everyone loved to eat the cherries.

Task
Tell a story about you doing something with seeds or pits like Bidemmi. Write your story to follow the pattern of *Cherries and Cherry Pits*.

Audience
You will read your story to the principal.

Purpose
Your principal will enjoy your story.

Procedure
1. Review the assessment lists.
2. Complete graphic organizer GO31.
3. Complete graphic organizer GO32.
4. Complete graphic organizer GO36.
5. Write your story.
6. Check your work with the assessment lists.

Figure 5.9a. Performance Task: Life Cycle

see the assessment lists on pages 162, 163, 164, and 165

Background
Bidemmi planted the cherry pit and it grew into a tree that had cherries to eat. Remember the beans we planted in the classroom?

Task
Draw the life cycles of the cherry and the bean. Write an explanation of how the two life cycles are the same.

Audience
You will send your pictures and writing to the science teacher at the high school.

Purpose
The science teacher will show your work to the high school science students. The high school students will be interested in your work.

Procedure
1. Review the assessment lists.
2. Use two copies of graphic organizer GO8 to draw the two life cycles.
3. Use graphic organizer GO41 to plan your explanation.
4. Write the explanation.
5. Check your work with the assessment lists.

Figure 5.8b. Performance Task Assessment List: Following the Example of Bidemmi (Graphic Organizer GO31)

1. Did I use at least four colors in my drawing of the setting?

Terrific   OK   Needs Work

2. Did I show many details?

Terrific   OK   Needs Work

3. Did I use foreground, middleground, and background?

Terrific   OK   Needs Work

4. Did I write descriptive words in each of the boxes?

Terrific   OK   Needs Work

Figure 5.8c. Performance Task Assessment List:
Following the Example of Bidemmi
(Graphic Organizer GO32)

1. Did I draw me as the main character?

Terrific   OK   Needs Work

2. Did I show many details?

Terrific   OK   Needs Work

3. Did I use at least four colors for emphasis?

Terrific   OK   Needs Work

4. Did I write descriptive words in each of the boxes?

Terrific   OK   Needs Work

Figure 5.8d. Performance Task Assessment List: Following the Example of Bidemmi (Graphic Organizer GO36)

1. Did I list the title, characters, setting, time, and place?

Terrific   OK   Needs Work

2. Did I plan the problem?

Terrific   OK   Needs Work

3. Did I plan the events that would take place in the story?

Terrific   OK   Needs Work

4. Did I describe the solution?

Terrific   OK   Needs Work

Figure 5.8e. Performance Task Assessment List: Following the Example of Bidemmi (Story)

1. Does the story present a problem and a solution?

Terrific   OK   Needs Work

2. Does my story describe the setting?

Terrific   OK   Needs Work

3. Does my story describe the main character?

Terrific   OK   Needs Work

4. Does my story use descriptive words?

Terrific   OK   Needs Work

Figure 5.9b. Performance Task Assessment List:
Cherry Life Cycle
(Graphic Organizer GO8)

1. Did I start with the cherry pit in space 1?

Terrific   OK   Needs Work

2. Did I show what happens to the cherry pit when it starts to grow in space 2?

Terrific   OK   Needs Work

3. Did I show what happens next in space 3?

Terrific   OK   Needs Work

4. Did I show the last part of the cherry life cycle in space 4?

Terrific   OK   Needs Work

Figure 5.9c. Performance Task Assessment List:
Bean Life Cycle
(Graphic Organizer GO8)

1. Did I show a bean in space 1?

     Terrific   OK   Needs Work

2. Did I show the bean when it starts to grow in space 2?

     Terrific   OK   Needs Work

3. Did I show what happens next in space 3?

     Terrific   OK   Needs Work

4. Did I show the last part of the bean life cycle in space 4?

     Terrific   OK   Needs Work

Figure 5.9d. Performance Task Assessment List: Life Cycle (Graphic Organizer GO41)

1. Did I plan a main idea about how the two life cycles are the same?

Terrific   OK   Needs Work

2. Did I plan three details about how the two life cycles are the same?

Terrific   OK   Needs Work

3. Did I plan to use the science vocabulary words?

Terrific   OK   Needs Work

4. Did I plan a conclusion about how the two life cycles are the same?

Terrific   OK   Needs Work

Figure 5.9e. Performance Task Assessment List:
Life Cycle (Explanation)

1. Does my explanation have a main idea about how the two life cycles are the same?

| Terrific | OK | Needs Work |

2. Did I write three details about how the two life cycles are the same?

| Terrific | OK | Needs Work |

3. Did I use descriptive words from the science vocabulary?

| Terrific | OK | Needs Work |

4. Did I check my spelling?

| Terrific | OK | Needs Work |

Figure 5.10a. Performance Task:
Amazing Webs
see the assessment lists on pages 167, 168, and 169

Background
You have learned about many kinds of spiders. There are many kinds of spider webs. What are some of the most amazing kinds of spider webs you studied?
Task
Draw a picture of the most amazing spider web you have seen.
Audience
Keep the picture in your spider folder for your Kindergarten Buddy.
Purpose
When your spider folder is complete, you will share it with your Kindergarten Buddy.
Procedure
1. Review the assessment lists.
2. Draw a picture of an amazing spider web.
3. Plan your explanation with graphic organizer GO41.
4. Write an explanation of how a spider web works.
5. Check your work with the assessment lists.

Figure 5.11a. Performance Task:
Spider Body Parts
see the assessment lists on pages 170, 171, and 172

Background
Spiders have body parts to help them catch and eat food. How does the spider use its body parts to catch and eat food?
Task
Draw a picture of a spider showing the details of its body parts.
Write an explanation of how it uses its body parts to catch and eat food.
Audience
Keep these pictures in your spider folder for your Kindergarten Buddy.
Purpose
When your spider folder is complete you will share it with your Kindergarten Buddy.
Procedure
1. Review the assessment lists.
2. Draw the picture.
3. Plan your writing with graphic organizer GO41.
4. Write the explanation.
5. Check your work with the assessment lists.

Figure 5.10b. Performance Task Assessment List: Amazing Webs (Drawing)

1. Did I draw an amazing spider web?

Terrific   OK   Needs Work

2. Did I draw the kind of spider that makes that kind of web?

Terrific   OK   Needs Work

3. Did I show how the spider web works?

Terrific   OK   Needs Work

4. Did I show the details?

Terrific   OK   Needs Work

Figure 5.10c. Performance Task Assessment List: Amazing Webs (Graphic Organizer GO41)

1. Did I plan a main idea about how a spider web works?

Terrific   OK   Needs Work

2. Did I plan three details about how the spider web works?

Terrific   OK   Needs Work

3. Did I plan a conclusion for my explanation about how a spider web works?

Terrific   OK   Needs Work

4. Is my work neat?

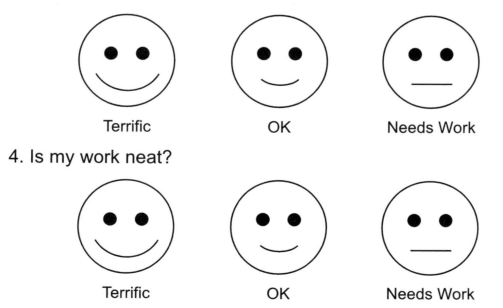

Terrific   OK   Needs Work

Figure 5.10d. Performance Task Assessment List: Amazing Webs (Explanation)

1. Did I write a main idea about how the spider web works?

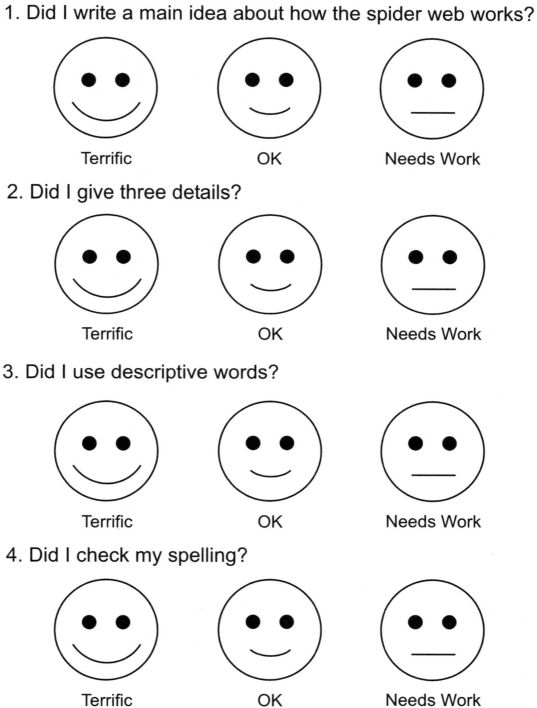

Terrific	OK	Needs Work

2. Did I give three details?

Terrific	OK	Needs Work

3. Did I use descriptive words?

Terrific	OK	Needs Work

4. Did I check my spelling?

Terrific	OK	Needs Work

Figure 5.11b. Performance Task Assessment List: Spider Body Parts (Drawing)

1. Did I draw a spider?

|Terrific|OK|Needs Work|

2. Does my drawing show the details of the spider's body parts?

Terrific   OK   Needs Work

3. Did I draw the body parts that help the spider catch and eat food?

Terrific   OK   Needs Work

4. Did I use color to emphasize the body parts used to catch and eat food?

Terrific   OK   Needs Work

Figure 5.11c. Performance Task Assessment List: Spider Body Parts (Graphic Organizer)

1. Did I plan a main idea about how the spider's body parts help it catch and eat food?

Terrific   OK   Needs Work

2. Did I plan at least three details about how the spider's body parts help it catch and eat food?

Terrific   OK   Needs Work

3. Did I plan to use the science vocabulary?

Terrific   OK   Needs Work

4. Did I plan a conclusion about how the spider's body parts help it catch and eat food?

Terrific   OK   Needs Work

Figure 5.11d. Performance Task Assessment List:
Spider Body Parts (Explanation)

1. Does my writing have an interesting main idea about how the body parts of a spider help it catch and eat food?

| Terrific | OK | Needs Work |

2. Did I use three supporting details to support my main idea?

| Terrific | OK | Needs Work |

3. Did I use the science vocabulary words?

| Terrific | OK | Needs Work |

4. Does my writing have an interesting conclusion?

| Terrific | OK | Needs Work |

Figure 5.12a. Performance Task:
Comparing Insects and Spiders

see the assessment lists on pages 174, 175, 176, and 177

Background

Some people think that insects and spiders are the same. But insects and spiders are alike in some ways and different in other ways.

Task

Make drawings to compare and contrast insects and spiders. Then plan and write an explanation of how insects and spiders are the same and how they are different.

Audience

Keep these pictures in your spider folder for your Kindergarten Buddy.

Purpose

When your spider folder is completed you will share it with your Kindergarten Buddy.

Procedure

1. Review the assessment lists.
2. Draw the pictures.
3. Use graphic organizer GO19 to compare and contrast insects and spiders.
4. Plan your writing with graphic organizer GO41.
5. Write the explanation.
6. Check your work with the assessment lists.

Figure 5.12b. Performance Task Assessment List: Comparing Insects and Spiders (Drawings)

1. Does my drawing show the details of the body parts of an insect?

Terrific   OK   Needs Work

2. Does my drawing show the details of the body parts of a spider?

Terrific   OK   Needs Work

3. Will my drawing help me compare and contrast insects and spiders?

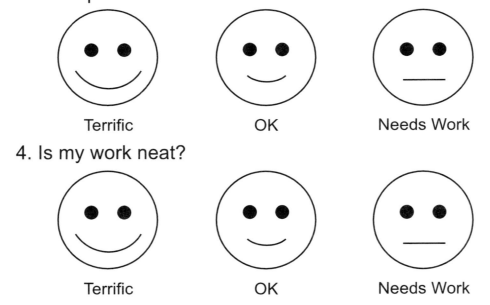

Terrific   OK   Needs Work

4. Is my work neat?

Terrific   OK   Needs Work

Figure 5.12c. Performance Task Assessment List:
Comparing Insects and Spiders
(Compare–Contrast Graphic Organizer)

1. Did I write the headings correctly?

Terrific   OK   Needs Work

2. Did I find at least three ways that insects and spiders are the same?

Terrific   OK   Needs Work

3. Did I find at least three ways that insects were unique?

Terrific   OK   Needs Work

4. Did I find at least three ways that spiders were unique?

Terrific   OK   Needs Work

Figure 5.12d. Performance Task Assessment List: Comparing Insects and Spiders (Graphic Organizer to Plan the Explanation)

1. Did I plan a main idea that would summarize how insects and spiders are the same and different?

Terrific   OK   Needs Work

2. Did I plan at least three details to support my main idea?

Terrific   OK   Needs Work

3. Did I plan the use of science vocabulary?

Terrific   OK   Needs Work

4. Did I plan a conclusion about how insects and spiders are the same and how they are different?

Terrific   OK   Needs Work

Figure 5.12e. Performance Task Assessment List: Comparing Insects and Spiders (Explanation)

1. Did I write an interesting main idea about how insects and spiders are the same and how they are different?

Terrific   OK   Needs Work

2. Did I use at least three details to support my main idea?

Terrific   OK   Needs Work

3. Did I use science vocabulary?

Terrific   OK   Needs Work

4. Did I write an interesting conclusion about how insects and spiders are the same and different?

Terrific   OK   Needs Work

Figure 5.13a. Performance Task:
Amazing Spiders

see the assessment lists on pages 179, 180, 181, 182, and 183

Background

What do you want to learn about spiders? Pick one of the following areas to research about spiders:

Spider Life Cycles

Spiders in the Food Chain

Where Spiders Live in the World

Spiders and People

Task

Ask research questions and find answers. Write a report. Draw illustrations for your report. You will put all of your work into a Spider Book.

Audience

You will share your Spider Book with your Kindergarten Buddy.

Purpose

Your Spider Book will help you teach your Kindergarten Buddy about spiders.

Procedure

1. Review the assessment lists.

2. Use graphic organizer GO40 to plan questions and summarize answers.

3. Use graphic organizer GO39 to evaluate the information sources on spiders

4. Plan your writing with graphic organizer GO41.

5. Write the report. Illustrate your report.

6. Check your work with the assessment lists.

7. Put your work together into your Spider Book.

8. Share your Spider Book with your Kindergarten Buddy.

Figure 5.13b. Performance Task Assessment List: Amazing Spiders (Planning Questions and Finding Answers)

1. Did I ask at least three questions?

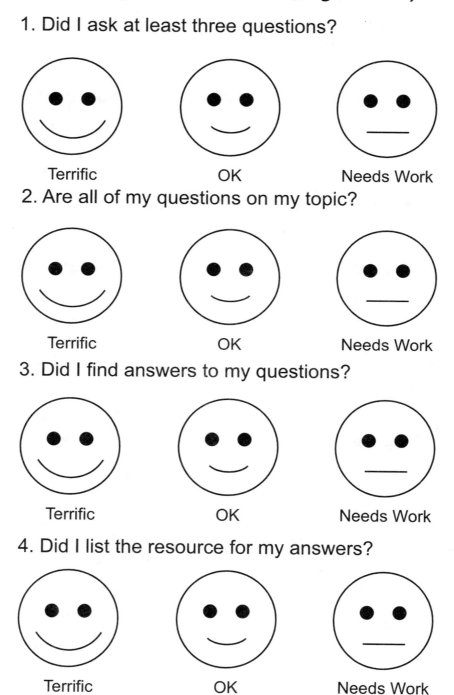

Terrific   OK   Needs Work

2. Are all of my questions on my topic?

Terrific   OK   Needs Work

3. Did I find answers to my questions?

Terrific   OK   Needs Work

4. Did I list the resource for my answers?

Terrific   OK   Needs Work

Figure 5.13c. Performance Task Assessment List: Amazing Spiders
(Evaluating Information Resources)

1. Did I complete an evaluation form for each of the information sources I used?

| Terrific | OK | Needs Work |

2. Did I complete all the parts of the evaluation forms?

| Terrific | OK | Needs Work |

3. Did I find some resources that were very good resources
   for my research?

| Terrific | OK | Needs Work |

4. Did I find some resources that were not good for my
   research? Did I explain why they were not good resources

| Terrific | OK | Needs Work |

Figure 5.13d. Performance Task Assessment List: Amazing Spiders (Collecting Information)

1. Did I write the questions I was trying to answer?

Terrific   OK   Needs Work

2. Did I list information for each question?

Terrific   OK   Needs Work

3. Did I show the sources of my information?

Terrific   OK   Needs Work

4. Did I put the books back where I found them?

Terrific   OK   Needs Work

Figure 5.13e. Performance Task Assessment List: Amazing Spiders (Planning the Report)

1. Did I plan a main idea about my research paper?

Terrific   OK   Needs Work

2. Did I plan at least one drawing in my report?

Terrific   OK   Needs Work

3. Did I plan to use details to support my main idea?

Terrific   OK   Needs Work

4. Did I plan a conclusion?

Terrific   OK   Needs Work

Figure 5.13f. Performance Task Assessment List: Amazing Spiders (Report)

1. Does my report have a clear main idea about my topic?

Terrific   OK   Needs Work

2. Does the illustration help me explain my main idea?

Terrific   OK   Needs Work

3. Did I use at least three supporting details to help explain my main idea?

Terrific   OK   Needs Work

4. Did I write an interesting conclusion?

Terrific   OK   Needs Work

References

Williams, V. B. (1986). *Cherries and Cherry Pits*. New York: William Morrow

Little Bear Books

Holmelund Minarik, E. (1957). *Little Bear* (pictures by Maurice Sendak). New York: HaperCollins.

Holmelund Minarik, E. (1960). *Little Bear's Friend* (pictures by Maurice Sendak). New York: HarperCollins.

Holmelund Minarik, E. (1961). *Little Bear's Visit* (pictures by Maurice Sendak). New York: HarperCollins.

Holmelund Minarik, E. (1996). *A Kiss for Little Bear* (pictures by Maurice Sendak). New York: HarperCollins.

Spiders

Generally, other books on spiders could be substituted for the titles listed here.

Back, C., & Watts, B. (1984). *Spider's Web*. Morristown, NJ: Silver Burdett.

Barret, N. (1989). *Spiders*. London: Franklin Watts.

Bason, L. (1974). *Spiders*. Washington, DC: National Geographic Society.

Beames, M. (1990). *The Little Spider* (J. Hurford, Illus.). Auckland, New Zealand: Shorthand Publications.

Berger, M., & Berger, G. (2000). *Do All Spiders Spin Webs?* (R. Osti, Illus.). New York: Scholastic.

Berman, R. (1998). *Spinning Spiders*. Minneapolis: Lerner Publications.

Chinery, M. (1991). *Spider*. Mahaw, NJ: Troll Associates.

Cole, J. (1995). *Spider's Lunch* (R. Broda, Illus.). New York: Grosset & Dunlap.

Gibbons, G. (1993). *Spiders*. New York: Scholastic.

Hawcock, D., & Montgomery, L. (1994). *Spider*. New York: Random House.

Hillyard, P. (1995). *Spiders and Scorpions* (S. Johnson, G. Slater, A. Pang, & A. Barrowman, Illus.). New York: Reader Digest Books.

Jones, C. (1996). *Spiders* (A. Palinay, Illus.). Huntington Beach, CA: Teacher Created Materials.

Krueger, C. (1992). *The Spider and The King* (B. Pollard, Illus.). Auckland, New Zealand: Shorthand Publications.

Llewellyn, C. (1997). *I Didn't Know That Spiders Have Fangs*. Brookfield, CT: Cooper Beech Books.

Lovett, S. (1991). *Extremely Weird Spiders*. Sante Fe, NM: John Muir Publications.

Merrians, D. (1997). *Spiders* (K. Kest, Illus.). New York: Troll Communications.

Patterson, P. J. (1992). *Spider Man*. Auckland, New Zealand: Shortland Publications.

Resnick, J. P. (1999). *Spiders*. Chicago: Kidsbooks.

Robinson, F. (1996). *Mighty Spiders!* (Day Zallinger, J., Illus.). New York: Scholastic.

Steedman, S. (Ed.). (1990). *Amazing Spiders*. New York: Alfred A. Knopf.

Winer, Y. (1998). *Spiders Spin Webs* (K. Lloyd-Jones, Illus.). Watertown, MA: Charlesbridge.